Tears of Fears

Believe

BEHIND CLOSED DOORS ...

Escaping the Abuse
AND
Discovering the Greatness within YOU!

The Solution for Women to Find the Power Within.

LADIES ... STOP THE INSANITY

It is time to change things in your life and for your life ...

By Lyn-Dee Eldridge aka ~Woobie~

Copyright © 2009 by Lyn-Dee Eldridge

All rights reserved. The materials in this book are provided for the personal use of the purchaser of the book. No redesign, editing, reproduction or creations of a derivative work from these materials is permitted without written permission of MasterMind Publishing, LLC. No part of this book may be used or reproduced in any manner whatsoever, including but not limited to, electronic, mechanical, photocopying, recording or otherwise, without written permission except for the inclusion of quotations in a review.

While it is the sincere intent of this publication to provide accurate and authoritative information in regard to the subject matter covered, the authors, publisher, and all those affiliated with the publication of this book, assume no responsibility for events occurring to any person or entity taking action or refraining from action as a result of the material in this publication.

Requests for permission to use any part of this book should be addressed to:
Lyn-Dee Eldridge
MasterMind Publishing, LLC
P.O. Box 549
Goffstown, NH 03045

To order the book go to http://www.tearsfears.com

Printed in United States of America

First printing 2008

ISBN 13: 978-0-9720941-0-8

ELDRIDGE, LYN-DEE,
  Tears of Fears Behind Closed Doors
        by Lyn-Dee Eldridge

Cover design and interior design/layout by Michele Bryant
www.michelesdesign.com • michele@michelesdesign.com •

Contents

Appreciation vii

Acknowledgements xi

Preface xiii

Personal Development xv

Bio – Warning xvii

Beginning Self-Help Exercise xix

Expressions xxi

"P.O.W." xxiv

About the Author xxv

Recommendations of Positive Music xxvii

Chapter 1

PART 1 The Beginning 1

PART 2 Biological Father 6

Chapter 2

PART 1 Getting Married to Prince Charming 13

PART 2 From Prince to ? 17

PART 3 Escaping Hell 22

PART 4 The Healing and Finding Out
        Who Are You? 27

PART 5	Back in Florida – The New Man	30
PART 6	The Control – Who Am I?	33
PART 7	Having a Baby	36
PART 8	Bringing the Baby Home and Happily Ever After ... Right	38
PART 9	The Final Straw	41

Chapter 3

PART 1	*FREE* & Single Parenting	45
PART 2	Being a Divorced Parent, Dealing with an Abusive Man ...	46

Chapter 4

PART 1	Sica had Enough ...	55
PART 2	Over the Rainbow – During the 20 years After the Divorce	56
PART 3	New Relationships	59

Chapter 5

PART 1	After Getting to Know Me	61
PART 2	Career/Problem With Being So Busy While Your Children Are Minors	62
PART 3	Kids Now Dating ...	64
PART 4	Sharing Some Other Nightmares	69

Chapter 6

PART 1 Finding Yourself 79
PART 2 Personal Development 82

Chapter 7

PART 1 And Through My Journey 85
Warning – Strong Lyn-Dee-ism 87

Epilogue

You Deserve Greatness and You Can Live 89
Poem 91
Your Healing Self-Help Exercise 93

Exercise Prescription

Day 1 and Then After 95
Morning 96
Evening 96
Daily 99

Legal Help

There is Help Legally 101

Appendix

PART 1 105
PART 2 106

we'll burn a candle to sooth our sorrows
and to cast the shadow of light
we'll spray our room with a sweet fragrance
to smell the sweet delight

just keep walking, just keep walking
allow no darkness to dim your sight
just keep walking, just keep walking
and follow that shadow of light

~~Woobie~~

Appreciation

Thanks to my family for all their support ...

First and foremost, I want to go out to my family for inspiring me to write my first book.

First to my husband, Mark ... you have put the word marriage back into the dictionary for me after 20 years of being divorced from an abusive man; you have given the definition of spouse a sweet meaning. You are my best friend and my soul mate; you are my inspiration and my prayer that came true. Thank you for being you and making a difference in so many ways. I love and adore you!

To our children: Sica, Ryan, Jason, and Sydney and our granddaughter, Briana. You are all so special. Thank you for allowing me to enjoy a great childhood through you. Thank you for the laughter and the brightness that children bring to the world. Thank you all for being unique and allowing me to not only support all of you in everything you do, but most importantly, be that friend that you can count on, not run from. You are all amazing in your own ways!

My family members are all walking in different chapters of life; Mark and I are now in our 40's; Sica in her 20's; Ryan and Jason in their mid-teens; Sydney, in her preteens; and Briana, 2 years old—just beginning to enter what we all call ... *the learning path to our future.*

To my children individually:

Sica, so many thanks go out to you. You are growing up to be an amazing inspiration to many and you don't even know it yet. You're a fantastic mom and I know the road ahead of you will be full of laughter, tears … (but tears of joy) and great success. Because of your willingness to help others, you have already started to pave a path of hope and light where others that follow are in the dark. *Thank you for our wonderful granddaughter, Briana!* But most importantly, thank you for giving me the strength to heal and move forward.

Ryan, you are a leader and you have many eyes that are watching you grow into a very strong young man; the world is all yours. Seize it! Whatever you choose to do in life, Dad and I love you and stand beside you every step of the way.

Jason, our jokester. You have some sense of humor! Always keeping us laughing; always ready for a great debate. Your strength, your powerful mind, and your determination will take you places others only wish they could go. You will always be leading by example and I know you will always make the right choices to succeed in whatever you want to do.

Sydney, you're so bright and special. You bring smiles to so many people you touch. I believe in you and I believe that you will be one of the most amazing women I know. You've got it all and more! Take it to the top and never allow anything to get in your way.

Briana, our little Miss Independent, already knows how to play it up and get her way ... you just warm every bone in my body and all I have to say is ... there is nothing like grandchildren to brighten up your day. Thank you for every day you brighten my life. Keep shining my angel, keep shinning. Woobie Loves You! (Woobie ... that's me. Woobie = warm, safe, cuddly and secure; that is the definition of who I am and that is my chosen name, as your grandma, Woobie.)

... To all my children, I love you all equally and hold each of you in my heart as if I carried each of you under my heart for nine months.

To my dear husband *Mark* *...* thank you for every morning that I awake to your warm whisper of "Good morning babe, I love 'ya," and the hug and kiss that jumpstart my day and thank you for your gentle embrace, kiss, and soft words that whisper from your lips every night, "Good night babe, I love 'ya." Thank you for being my best friend. I love 'ya ;) *get in the truck...*

To all of our hotline consultants at the abuse centers nationwide that are always picking up the phone and donating their time, no matter what time it is 24/7, 365 days a year. Thank you for being there for all of us. Thank you for your willingness to listen and your gentle voice to get us through our living hell. Thanks for all you do and the difference you help create within ourselves! To all the volunteers and staff at all the help centers around the world for all you do ~ A BIG thank you! ☺. If there are such things as angels … you all wear the wings G-D[1] Bless You!

A very special thanks to my dear friends, the ladies whose stories I shared but left their names out; I love you and we all appreciate you. You are amazing women & survivors.

And last but not least, Thank you, my readers, for allowing me to pour myself into you. This book is all about how to help you become YOU!

---

[1] In keeping with Jewish tradition, when I reference the Lord, it will appear as G-D.

Acknowlegements

Jean Sutton You've always inspired me since the first time we met at the prime rib restaurant in Orlando, 2004! Thanks for taking time to be the first to proof read my book and help correct my booboo's. I feel better.

Michele Bryant for all your talents that just added a wonderful calming and soothing effect with your creative artistic abilities. I applaud you for your commitment to meet a deadline even thru one of your most challenging times!

Linda Parker for her willingness to jump in and grab the bull by the horns and help at the drop of a dime. And your guidance to making my book as powerful as possible for all women young and old.

Paige Ragan We have never even met or spoken, but you were on call and ready to jump in.

Elsom Eldridge Jr. for *your* incredible support and knowledge that have opened many doors for me and being my guardian angel.

Mark L. Eldridge for all your time you dedicated to research and helping me in every way

Andrew Goodwin When you touch canvas, it comes alive! I appreciate all the time and thought you contributed.

www.tearsfears.com

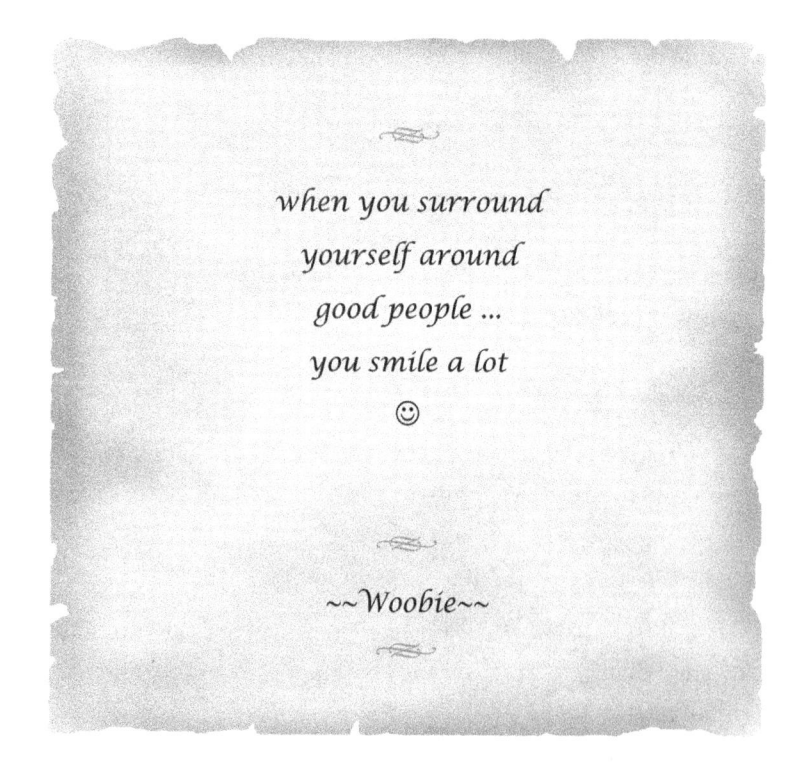

when you surround
yourself around
good people ...
you smile a lot
☺

~~Woobie~~

Preface

*T**he Solution for Finding **the** Power Within is to Listen, Accept, Receive, and Take Action ...*

I dedicate this book to *You*.

I dedicate this book to you. You need to know, you are not alone; your pain is felt by many, and I want to reach out to you. I want you to realize there is a light at the end of each tunnel and through all your chapters of life, there comes experiences; you become wiser, more knowledgeable and it helps you learn new things about you that make you stronger and better.

As you read this book, I have chosen it to be read as if I was speaking to you ... with you. What I write, may not always be politically correct in publishing terms, but it is politically correct in Lyn-Dee-ism terms. I go out to you in hopes you will understand you are not alone; there are many just like you, the only difference is ... your name and face, and outer shell ... but we all share similar if not the same nightmares and dreams.

Also, it is not an error if you read things that are printed more than once throughout this book. I believe there are times we need to re-read and absorb some statements more than once in different areas to help us grow through these situation.

I will not be going into great details of the abuse I personally have experienced; I don't feel that is necessary. We all understand what abuse is, being beaten down mentally and physically, to the extreme of losing your own identity.

Personal Development

At the end of my abusive marriage, I kept hearing about this *'Personal Development'* stuff and then I decided to look into it and I am so glad I did.

Let this be one of your healing exercises you do every day ...

I highly recommend you start this for yourself *today*. You don't need any money to have access to great books and/or listen to great audios. You can go to the library to get the books and audios and you can go on the Internet to www.youtube.com for great Personal Development, so if money is an issue, no worries. If money is not an issue, start your own Personal Development home library. Personal Development will help you change your life for the better and find the *greatness within yourself*. It will give you the strength and the direction to move forward everyday.

It's amazing how you can truly find yourself through self-improvement, motivational products. There is so much negativity in the world today. Every day we are faced with it one way or another, inside our home and outside, and that is why it is important that you do this personal development exercise every day, whether it is reading ten pages from a good book and/or listening for at least fifteen minutes to a good audio tape.

I cannot stress enough how important this is to do and try to never skip a day. Maybe do this right before bed, and/or listen to it on your way to work or when you are going somewhere in your car. Stop watching TV for a little while and replace it with your personal development time. You truly need to do this every day for yourself and you will be so glad you did.

To name a few Personal Development Mentors, here are a few suggestions of authors for you to look up.

- Les Brown

- Zig Ziglar

- Jim Rohn

- Robert Kiyosaki

- Paul J. Meyer

- Jeff Olson – "The Slight Edge"

Bio – Warning

*P*lease allow me to take a moment and go out to my biological family ... so I don't surprise or shock or hurt them with my words from this point on.

What you're about to read is my side of the story. I have forgiven all of you for the hurt and the pain that I carry within me. My words come from the wisdom and the experience and that is how and why I'm able to help others go through what most call Hell. So as you read on, be proud of me ... not mad at me. I am grateful for all the good, bad, and hurtful experiences that I have had in my life, it has made me who I am today ... I do love all of you; after all, you are my bio.

Mom, I do realize, you were the mother you thought was best. I know I wasn't a complete angel growing up and there were times you needed to discipline me, but to the extreme you did ... was not necessary nor deserved. And your words to me were so painful ... but you never gave them a second thought, they were just repeated. To my siblings ... I know as you read on ... you will remember and agree.

As you read on, please realize I am not crying or whining ... I'm expressing, sharing, and now smiling = making a positive

TEARS OF FEARS BEHIND CLOSED DOORS

difference in helping so many; helping them have strength and hope to move forward. And at the same time, allowing me to once again, empty my bucket of emotional pain.

Beginning Self-Help Exercise

(Recommended to have — a long door mirror)

Every time you are doing this self-help exercise, please listen to these songs as you are standing or sitting in front of your mirror:

Mary J. Blig's, *"Just Fine"*

Ryan Shupe & The Rubberbands, *"Dream Big"*

Before we get started, please go look into the mirror and see who you are right now … take a good look, (this might take you a moment or several minutes, may be even an hour(s)) and understand I have been there too. Look inside yourself and if you are asking your image …"What happened to you? Who are you? When did I lose you?" … I understand.

I hope by the time you are done reading this book, you will go back to the mirror and look at yourself and believe you have been found and you are ready to enjoy your new journey of life.

Expressions

Tears of Fears
Behind Closed Doors ...

Do You Believe....!

You are Someone Special

The Solution for Finding the Power Within is to

Listen, Except, Receive and Take Action…

All it takes is the strength and the desire from the

passion in words of wisdom … that are spoken to

you through experience … and you then believe in

yourself … for whom you truly are.

You now have been found! Now follow the light!

~~Woobie~~

Do the one thing you think you cannot do.
Fail at it. Try again.
Do better the second time.
The only people who never tumble are
those who never mount the high wire.
This is your moment. Own it.

~~ Oprah Winfrey ~~
9/8/86
The Oprah Winfrey Show Debuts

AND ONE FINAL NOTE BEFORE WE GET STARTED …

I will go ahead and apologize now
if ever throughout this book, I offend you …
with that being said … I am Lyn-Dee …
there will be times when a Lyn-Dee-ism
will escape here and there and some of my
suggestions might be a little, shall we say …
to the point and a shocker to you … but again,
I can assure you, it is not meant to be offensive …,
if it offends you, ignore it,
it wasn't meant for you,
it was meant for my other readers!
LOL

Now, let's get started …

Believe that we all have the Power within ourselves:

"P.O.W."

POWER OF WHAT IF ...　　(I Can Do it)

POWER OF WANT ...　　(I Can Do it)

POWER OF WOMEN ...　　(I Can Do it)

POWER OF WITHIN ...　　(I Can Do it)

You can do anything you set your mind to ...

... ANYTHING!

About The Author

We live in a world that is sometimes not so colorful, not so fair and sometimes what we think to be a dead-end street. Everyone has the right to live; no one should feel as if they are a failure or be told what they are capable of doing and not doing. Everyone has the right to create a lifestyle that they dream about. I have been where you are, in a very dark and lonely place.

I hope through this book, I am in so many ways, able to reach out and touch you so you will find yourself and the greatness within you. It is because of my dark and lonely past, that I can now sleep peacefully at night, knowing everyday I have helped another person and family smile and heal!

Recommendations Of Positive Music

During your journey through this book ...

There are millions of songs of wisdom and strength that are inspiring and uplifting that we relate to every day.

Two of the songs that recently inspired me are listed below. I am sharing this with you because for this book, I would like to recommend that you listen to these two songs, (I have them both on a CD and on my iPOD).

When I need some great inspiration and a charge, I have been listening to them ... they are always there with me. Sometimes I cry, most of the time now I smile and sing aloud.

These are the two songs that really stuck in my head as I was writing this book and I believe them to be very powerful. I highly recommend that you listen to "DREAM BIG" and "JUST FINE" at the beginning of this book, during, and at the end.

I believe that you will feel the same as I do when you listen to these songs. The feeling of hope and 'I can accomplish anything I believe in'. Sit back and just absorb the words; cry if you need to … smile when you can, but always remember … Believe in yourself!

"Dream Big" song lyrics by Ryan Shupe & The Rubberbands can be found on the Internet.

"Just Fine" song lyrics by Mary J. Blige can be found on the Internet.

CHAPTER 1

PART ONE
The Beginning

*A*s I start writing this book, I will begin from day one of my life ... Some of you have had a better beginning, some worse, but this is mine ...

I was born October 22, 1960, 8:40 AM in New York. My parents already had two children: Ira, age six and Ronda, age four. There were problems with my parent's marriage before me and after me, maybe they thought I would be the cure ... but I wasn't ... if anything I was told and made to feel as if I was a **big mistake**.

Now picture this, in the early 60's, Jewish couple lived in Jericho, N.Y.; I believe doing pretty well financially, nice house, my mother was spoiled with furs and such; she didn't work, had a maid/nanny. My father owned his own business; things looked pretty good from the outside. You know the house with the

2   TEARS OF FEARS BEHIND CLOSED DOORS

white picket fence — The Perfect Family!

But then in 1961 they got divorced ... (when divorce was taboo). Jewish woman left with three children and 'wow' was she angry and very bitter; they divorced when I was a year old. I never got to know my father as I was growing up. Well, little bits and pieces of him here and there ... I was always told and reminded that he was a *"No good son of a bitch."*

Now mind you, my father was not a faithful husband and cheated on my mother a lot. My mother had every right to be angry and hurt. However, she didn't have the right to poison us kids against my father!

Shortly after the divorce, my mother, brother, sister, and I moved to Bellrose, New York to live with my grandmother. The five of us lived in a very small three-bedroom apartment in Glen Oaks. My grandmother was a strong, independent European woman from Hungary. My grandmother hated the world, but adored her grandchildren. She and my Uncle Izzy were the only ones who truly showed me love, but with my mother ruling the house, my grandmother and my uncle could only do so much.

My aunt (mother's sister) and uncle (Uncle Izzy) lived just around the corner from us. My uncle was wonderful. They had three children, all boys ... I was my uncle's little girl and I loved him dearly. But there was a problem. When I was growing up, my mother would fight with her sister 90 percent of the time, which then turned around to them not speaking for years and once again. Because my mother wasn't speaking to my aunt and uncle, I was forbidden to see, speak, or have any contact with

CHAPTER ONE

my uncle And if I did sneak to see my uncle, the punishment was severe. So the two people in my life growing up who would show me love and acceptance, were limited to being a part of my life. How sad!

Please, don't do this to your children ... If there are good people that can be a part of their lives, let them be a part of their lives. You don't have to agree with everything or everyone, as long as it's not a traumatic problem ... then deal with the kids getting well-rounded and having positive people in their lives. My mother and her sister would argue over the stupidest things ... I remember it one time being over sugar.

There wasn't a week that went by that I wasn't abused mentally and/or physically in my house. We were now poor and just getting by. My brother and sister were not the nicest to be around and they made it perfectly clear, I was in the way. My sister, being treated as the princess, and my brother at a very young age, being the man of the house ... or so he thought. He would beat me and my sister was like the wicked stepsisters you see on Cinderella. I was told more often than not, I was ugly, stupid, a big mistake, and useless and I should only wish I was more like my sister who was smart, talented, pretty, and had a lot going for her. (Allow me to share with you that today in our adult years we are closer and much more civil to one another.)

Living in a house that there was no love for me, with the exception of my grandmother, Julia, it was empty and lonely. My childhood life just wasn't warm and fuzzy. (woobie, is what I like to call it. woobie = warm, safe, secure, cozy.)

It was lonely and dark. My mother and siblings showed me hate and anger and that no way, did I belong in their space. My siblings followed what my mother did to me and it was allowed. I share this with you … just so you know; I understand what "no love" is.

Now, I wasn't always an angel, I'll admit that. I grew up very independent, a tomboy, and very New York Street Smart. I would stand my ground if I felt I was right (but only outside my house). I loved people, but hated to be bullied outside my house. I loved my friends.

I never considered my family to be my best friends, you know, the ones you can go to for anything … in fact it was just the opposite. No matter what happened in the house, it was always my fault and I was beaten for it. (Today, we know it as child abuse; everything from the belt (buckle), to a stick, to a spoon, to an electrical cord, to bites on my face, and even beaten with a pole.) So why bother?

Thank G-D for my friends who were on the other side of the door. My friends were my family; they were my home away from home. They showed me love, acceptance, support, and laugher. They knew who I was and didn't expect anything more or less of me.

So if you had a dark childhood, I understand. How I have come to be the woman I am today and to be able to reach out to you is because I've never regretted anything that has happened to me … it all made me who I am today.

CHAPTER ONE 5

Please never regret. Just grow from it.

When I was eleven years old, my mother married a wonderful man who saw what had been done to me in the years that had passed and he did help change things to a certain degree. However, the scars were inside me and the abuse still continued. We then moved to South Florida in 1972 and started our *new* lives. (Or they did ... I was just transplanted.)

My teenage years were not as bad, still the same in many ways. I was definitely independent, strong-minded, always said what was on my mind, and stood up for everything I believed in. Sometimes that brought challenges into my life, but for the most part as I was growing up, my family was changing their ways about me and toward me. Not to the conclusion that made me feel any closer to them, they just, I guess, couldn't bully me as much anymore as the years went on.

I started to work at the age of 12 and I now could have some financial independence and didn't have to ask for the things I wanted/needed. In school, I was very well liked and everyone knew that whatever I said or did, there was no nonsense about it. Very few knew about my home life. None of my friends were ever allowed over ... my siblings could bring home whomever they wanted ... but that wasn't the case for me. We lived in a beautiful 4-bedroom house in Florida, but I still didn't have my own room; I shared a room with my grandmother. The room that was supposed to be shared with my sister and I, was all about my sister; her posters were hung on the wall, everything was about her. I wasn't allowed to hang anything on the walls, arrange the room the way I would have liked to, so there wasn't a place for me. Whatever went on behind closed doors, stayed behind closed doors.

PART TWO
Biological Father

Here is what I want to share with you if you have a child(ren). Just because the father of your child(ren) isn't (wasn't) the man he should have been to you or even the father he should have been to your child(ren), even if there was/is mental and/or physical abuse, just protect them the best you can. You don't have to poison the kids with thoughts that he is a, "no good s.o.b.," they will see through the truth one day and make up their own minds and opinions and see him for what he truly is … allow the kids to make up their own minds about their biological father.

I promise you this; your child(ren) will see their father for whom he truly is, (my daughter did). If you have to talk about him and the children are around, (it doesn't matter if they are in the same room or a different room), if you know they are around, anywhere, they will and do hear you. Unless they are 100% away from you and cannot walk in to hear or see you, please think twice about what you are saying about their father. Make up a different name for the father of your child(ren), I did, I called him *ANUS*.

My ex-husband's name is Joe, and I have chosen not to use his given birth name for the remainder of my book; he only deserves

CHAPTER ONE

to be recognized by his nick name. This nickname just fit and is so perfect! (You can use it if you want and it fits your ANUS, LOL!) And my daughter never knew who I was talking about, EVER. Now she is 23, a single mom, and I had shared this with her just recently so she too, doesn't poison her daughter.

Something to think about ... If you take away your child(ren's) daddy, you are setting them up for, "looking for love in all the wrong places." What do I mean? When your child(ren) grow up and start to date, it is inevitable that any guy that shows them any kind of affection, starting with the first smile and hug, they will feel the love, which can set them up for excepting the abuse that might follow. (Not always ... but think about that ...)

If they can have a strong father figure in their lives, the chances are more likely that they will not be desperate for the love and they will be choosier of their choice in men and have a lot more self-esteem and confidence. Again, this is not always the case, but something to think about and ponder.

If your child(ren) are the product of an abusive father or a father that had disappeared out of their lives, please be aware of the signs of low self-esteem and having no confidence within themselves and get them professional help. Suggest they call a hotline whenever they need to vent and as they are growing-up, try to help them the best you can. It is hard sometimes to see the signs, just be there for them, and support them through their hard times, especially when they are teenagers and know it all. (Life is not easy for them or you!)

As for my father, he was *not allowed* to see us, speak to us, or send us anything. I do recall him coming by when I was five-ish and it didn't go over very well at all. That was the last time I saw him until I was eight. It was as if he was dead or should have been. If I ever mentioned his name ... watch out ... mother's fangs would come out!

I was one of those kids growing up that when I watched TV, I'd watch, *My Three Sons, Father Knows Best, Family Affair, Leave it to Beaver*; I would cry for a daddy, (I learned to cry silently so I wouldn't get hit). That was back in the day, when television only had four stations: 4, 6, 10, and 33.

My mother would date and I remember them taking my siblings places, but driving off and leaving me behind. I was shut out of the family activities only to be told I didn't belong.

At the age of eight, we got a call from my father who was living in California with his wife and they invited us three kids to come and see them and spend one month with them. Keep in mind we have been poisoned all these years about this, *"no good s.o.b.."* My brother wanted no part of him, but my sister and I wanted to go and did.

Now, I was, I admit, the brat from hell! ... A parent's worst nightmare. This "no good son of a bitch," owed me big time, was my thinking and I came off as such. Needless to say, it was the vacation from hell for all of us. Looking back on it, I am ashamed of how I acted and treated them. The vacation that was supposed to last one month was cut short and we were sent back to New York after two weeks, never to see or hear from my father until later years. Long story short, there were a few times I tried to re-unite, but things (people) got in the way. Ugly stories

CHAPTER ONE

were told to him about me that weren't true from a few people, because they didn't want him to be a part of me or get to know me (I will keep this drama out of my book). Just realize there are people in your lives that just will try to get in your way ... plow through them.

But life is funny, and here is the #1 reason why I don't want you to share your feelings with your children. Never have your kids ever look at you as if you kept them from their father. It will come back to you and bite you. Never allow your issues to interfere with their rights to know their biological parent. Here is why I shared this with you ... from my own experience and knowing others that grew up without one of their parents, it is inevitable, and curiosity kills the cat. No matter what, no matter how bad the father was/is ... a child will always get to the age, usually around 18, where they want to know and see their biological parent. Good, bad, or indifferent, they want to meet them and see for themselves.

If you allow them to make up their own minds and gain their own opinions, they will see them for whom they truly are. (I will share with you a little later what happened with my daughter and her father).

As for my father and me, I resent and hold it against my mother that I never got to know my dad, never got to laugh and play with him, never got to get the love that a daddy gives his little girl, and wasn't able to have a dad growing up. I resent all of it! I will never forgive my mother for that, or I should say, I forgave her, I just never forgot.

When I did finally meet my father, he was wonderful! I feel as if that part of my life was stolen and it can never be replaced or fulfilled. I feel as if I had been robbed ... and you know what, *I was.* (Please, don't do this to your children.) By the time we met, the father-daughter relationship was too late to have, but the friendship that we grew to have was priceless.

It wasn't until I was in my mid 30's when I got to meet my father in Colorado and really got to know the man that somehow I was so much like. How weird is that, never grew up with him, but I have so many traces of him it is uncanny. And you know what, he really enjoyed me as well and said it himself; he could kick himself for listening to other people who he allowed to steal our relationship. This is something that can never be given back. He was a wonderful, kind, and a caring man. It was great having him in my life and my daughter's life.

It was a long distance relationship, as I lived in Florida and he in California, so we would speak on the phone and got in a few visits. But what I thought would be a great future with my father, was cut very short as he passed away five short years later after we re-united for the last time.

My father was diagnosed with cancer and was told he only had six months to live. And in the sixth month, he passed. When I told my mother that he was passing away, she told me I shouldn't speak to him ever again, that she felt slighted and how dare he come into my life and try to be a parent now! @#$%^&* (I still to this day, cannot figure that one out?)

In so many ways, I took after my father. He was very active;

CHAPTER ONE

loved people, loved doing things, always going and loving life, not selfish and a hard worker. He would always help those that were willing to help themselves and would never turn his head if he saw something was going on and it was wrong. He would stand for what he believed in and appreciated everything from the breeze in the air to the thunderstorm that lit up the sky. Very positive, motivated person.

What a shame I never really got to know him. However, I appreciate the time we had.

The child within us is walking alone
Searching for a part of them to
find their own

Through the years and the journeys

and all that be said

Comes the adult that is
searching
for the greatness ahead...

~~Woobie~~

CHAPTER 2

PART ONE

GETTING MARRIED TO PRINCE CHARMING

Let's step back and then fast forward so I can get to the part that means so much to me and that is truly reaching out to you. I just have to share my past so you understand I am right beside you, OK?

At the age of 18, on Saturday, June 30, 1979, at 6 PM, I got married to a man that was wearing the nice guy, perfect husband, best friend disguise. You know what I am talking about. He was funny, warm, nice, considerate, well liked … What a Guy! And he was until we moved to Montgomery, Alabama due to a job transfer for him in August 1979.

14 TEARS OF FEARS BEHIND CLOSED DOORS

Allow me to paint the picture of my ex-husband, Anus. Outside the house, people thought he was "*The Man.*" He worked in a Catholic hospital in Montgomery, Alabama and he was very, *very* well liked by the nuns, the priest, and the staff. He went to church every Sunday and I even went with him. He was known as the man every woman wanted to have. I was told several times, how lucky I was to have him. He came across as a very hard worker and a very dedicated employee ... valued by many.

Our home: We lived in a two bedroom, one bath apartment that was cute. Our home was spotless, you could, as they say, eat off my floor, and that was no exaggeration. He would leave the house at 10:30 AM and get home around 8 PM. Life was still good and very comfortable, secure.

Because of how I was brought up, my parents being divorced and being raised without a father, I never wanted to get divorced. I was going to be married to him for the rest of my life. No matter what, I dedicated everything to him (and he knew it).

At the age of 18, I was the perfect wife, (learning to cook), so I cooked, cleaned, ironed, and the house was his castle. Anus is ten years older than I am. I took being his wife very seriously and I was mature for my age. He would come home and everything was done for him. And, I loved doing it all; I didn't look at it as if this was something that was forced on me to do, I truly loved being a wife and I loved working and going to school. I can honestly say I felt as if my life was fulfilled. Looking back now, I realize it wasn't; what I mean by that, is I did everything just so I didn't have to hear him complain. He molded me and I didn't even know it was happening. Moral to this reality is, *never* do things just because you are worried about what your partner is going to say or do.

Don't allow your past to dictate your present, or your present to dictate and halt your future. It is time to stand up for yourself and determine what you will and will not allow.

I had a job at the same hospital. Then I decided to go to cosmetology school. That was awesome! So I worked and went to school and was the housewife. As a woman, I could and did handle everything very well.

Even though I worked and went to school, still dinner was always ready for him when he walked in the door. Not fast food either, a full course meal, starting with salad all the way to dessert. House was clean and laundry always done.

I never saw the abuse coming, nor did I know it was happening. You know what I am talking about.

I never understood how I would allow this to happen until it was over seven years later, so don't you dare, think you are stupid or question how could you allow it to happen to you now. We might walk strong on the outside, but we are weak on the inside, desperate for their love and appreciation. Always justifying why things are happening and why your partner is acting the way he is. The mental abuse … the invisible abuse, you cannot and do not see it, feel it, nor do you believe it is happening.

Here is what I know as I look back at my abusive past with my ex, there were signs, but I didn't see them as my future to hell,

16   TEARS OF FEARS BEHIND CLOSED DOORS

I was blind by wanting to make him happy, putting him first, wanting acceptance, and then just wanting him not to *complain* about anything *all* the time.

Please allow me to help you shed some light on how it happens to us. SLOWLY and INVISIBLY.

First of all, physical abuse, you can feel it coming and you can see it coming. It doesn't take a genius to realize you are about to get hit. I know plenty of women that have gone through or are going through physical abuse and it is so sad and scary to witness this.

As a matter of fact, my ex tried to hit me, once meaning to and the second time, I am not sure if he meant to or if it was an accident, anyway, twice. The first time, we were standing in the hallway of our condo in Florida, before we moved to Alabama. I don't know what I said to annoy him, or if I even said anything at all … maybe it was something that happened before he came home … not sure, but he closed his fist and swung at me. HELLO! I could see it coming and with that, (being the tomboy that I was growing up and being New York Street Smart), I pushed him so hard that he hit the closet doors and bounced back at me, and I remember pushing him a couple of times because I just couldn't believe he was going to hit me. HE NEVER TRIED IT AGAIN!

And the other time when we were leaving a wedding where he came off as Mr. Personality, good Catholic boy married to a Jew. He allowed his boss at the time to belittle me and humiliate me in front of a room full of people in regard to me being Jewish. I was hurt and offended that my husband did not stand up for me. We were driving home and I will never forget it; I was wearing a blue dress and he always wore, (probably still does), a raised ring that looked like J. C. I still to this day, believe he didn't mean to hit me, I think he was just throwing his hands up as to say, "What the f---", but he cocked me in my eye, just below my eyebrow and the blood just poured out of me. In fear of what he did, he was yelling at me ... long story short, I had a concussion. That was the last time he ever laid a hand on me.

As this story goes on: Whenever Anus introduced me to anyone, he would always label me ... "This is my wife, Lyn-Dee, she's Jewish." Why ... I don't know, I guess he thought it was cute, funny at first (only to him) and then I guess it became a habit to say it. Why? Because he was an Anus.

PART TWO
*F*rom *P*rince *T*o ?

I was blinded by the abuse coming into my life.

He had multiple personalities but no one knew it; hell I didn't even know it.

We moved to Alabama, and shortly after (now check this out, why wasn't this a sign to me?), he met a few people that belonged to the KKK (Ku Klux Klan). In Alabama, the KKK was very well known for their presence. In the early 80's, they would march through towns and it was known they were there. He decided he wanted to become a member. HELLO! Your wife is Jewish, Anus! Needless to say, I wasn't happy. When I saw the application on the dining room table, I was speechless. He said, "I don't have to tell them I am married to a Jew." My reply, "But you are and aren't you a good Catholic guy?" To this day, I have no idea if he ever filled out the application or not.

But that should have been the start of the clue that this guy, just wasn't right.

And how many times have you heard …

You're ugly, who would want you?
You're fat, who would want you?
You're stupid, who would want you?
Where the hell are you going, you couldn't make it without me
You can't do anything right
You're pregnant, who would want you?
Who would want you, you have a baby … no one would
  even look at you
Don't do it that way, do it this way …
You can't wear that …
You can't do that …
You can't … You can't … You can't …
Does this sound familiar? …

I heard it so much that I believed it. I said, "I'm sorry," for things I didn't even do or was responsible for happening. *(Sound familiar?)* I said, "I'm sorry" to everyone, even if I didn't cause whatever happened. People would say to me, "You have no reason to

CHAPTER TWO

be sorry, stop saying that," and I would say ... "I'm sorry." *(Sound familiar?)*

Without going into great details of all the times I was told the things above and bought into his nonsense, I became even more insecure and very lonely, once again.

I would look into the mirror and spit at myself, I thought of my reflection as ugly and not good enough. I would hate everything about me, I would always try to do what he said was right and when I did, I was told I did it wrong. Sound familiar?

Home was spotless; so he would come home and flick his ash from his cigarette on the carpet, and say, "The carpet needs to be vacuumed," so I got out the vacuum cleaner. Dinner would be hot when he came home, but he would wait to eat and then yell at me for it being cold. We didn't have microwaves back then so reheating food wasn't so easy. Then he would complain that the dinner was overcooked.

He would have make-believe friends who said they saw me talking to a guy or looking at a guy and I wasn't even where he said it happened. He became very jealous, controlling, and very possessive.

We would be in the car going somewhere, and if I were just looking out the window, he would accuse me of looking at some guy. WHAT GUY? WHERE? I was just looking out the window. It became so annoying to me, that when we were in the car, I would look down and only down. Then he would say, look at the _____ and I would look up and then what do you think he would say ... Yep, "Do you like that guy, do you want to meet him, why are you looking at him?" bla bla bla ... *(Sound familiar?)*

He would throw things on the kitchen floor and tell me there was a mess in the kitchen.

I had a wonderful dog I rescued. Anus would throw a ball at my dog because he knew it would make me crazy to see that he was trying to hit her. He would actually call her out from the room because she would hide when he came home and then throw the ball at her.

He bought me a 38 Special Smith and Wesson gun on one of my birthdays and told me now I can go and blow my brains out.

He bought me a knife set on one of the holidays so I should stab myself.

He would take my car so I wouldn't be able to go anywhere.

He would tell me we were going out, to go get dressed and look nice ... and when I did ... he said he changed his mind, we're not going, go get undressed.

Any of these sound familiar?

However, on the other side of the door, no one knew of the abuse. They only knew if they became friends and came over. And even then, he would make jokes and at first, everyone thought he was funny, 'what a guy,' and then the more people got to be around him (us), they saw the true Anus.

Too many people that saw what was going on, would tell me

CHAPTER TWO

to leave, I didn't deserve any of this abuse ... but how? Man, I wanted to leave, but I was scared and not sure where or what or how *(Sound familiar?)* And thinking I failed at my marriage was absolutely devastating to me.

I'll never forget when my sister and her husband and their 15-month-old baby boy drove up to Alabama from South Florida to see me and they were going to stay for two weeks. We had a guest room so they were staying with us. Anus was so rude and mean to me and them, they cut their trip in half and left after one week, begging me to leave with them.

This was funny, he would complain because the baby would eat a cookie and get crumbs on the floor ... and I don't know how the baby knew to do this, but it was priceless. The last morning they were there and they were getting ready to hit the road back to Florida and Anus was leaving for work ... the baby, took a chocolate chip cookie and put it inside his shoe. No one knew the baby did this until he slipped on his shoe and it was the funniest thing when he said, "What the f---", and pulled his foot out of his shoe and saw the crumbled cookie. He was furious and he stormed out and we all just laughed hard and we enjoyed every moment of it. *Paybacks are a _____!*

There were many, many times things went on, but like I said at the beginning of my book, I don't have to go into all the details of all the times when the abuse took place, just know you are not alone.

This has been going on for two years now ... TWO YEARS of my life. (How long has it been for you?) If it has been more than a day, it has been going on long enough.

PART THREE
Escaping Hell

On April 14, 1982, it was time to escape. I was scared and very nervous, but I knew I had to get out of the hell I was living. I was going crazy and I mean crazy. I didn't want to live anymore and I was trying to figure out a way how to end this horrible life … I would sit in my rocking chair in my bedroom that was by the window and pull my hair out, one strand at a time and just cry. I would grab my skin on my arms and twist it and I remember even biting myself on the arm just to feel a different pain then the heaviness on my heart. *(Any of this sound familiar?)* And I would cry and ask myself, "Why is this happening to me, why is he doing this to me, how could he treat me so badly, what else can I do to fix this?" *(Sound familiar?)*

I had a friend named George who lived upstairs from us with his wonderful wife, Debbie. George was beside himself when he would witness the abuse. He told me if there was anything he could do to help me get out, just let him know.

Well, finally I crumbled … I was leaving. I had to get out of there. I called my mother in Florida and told her I need help. I need to get out of here, I need to leave with my dog, (Sweeties was her nick name, Bama Sweet Inspiration was her full name and she was a sweet inspiration, a beautiful black Cocker Spaniel, four years old that was once a show dog.) I couldn't leave my dog behind, so with that cry for help, my family helped me.

CHAPTER TWO 23

I got a one-way ticket to fly back to Florida with my dog for three weeks later. Now the process of leaving …

I needed to plan this out right so I could leave and not be pulled back in. I was *running away* and with the help of my friend George, I was able to pack and store things a little at a time so Anus didn't know. He loved the arcades, they were big in the early 80's. George would take him to the arcades and call me 15 minutes before they would be heading back home to give me enough notice to have the apartment together as if I wasn't packing. (I packed things that he wouldn't notice, things that were in the closets, in storage, things that meant a lot to me that he wouldn't see as being gone). As I packed, I took inventory of the things that were in sight and would be missed if I packed them, so those things were saved for the final hour before I was going to leave … I had made a list.

☙ Again, I repeat, as I packed, I also took inventory of what I needed to take the last day and made a list. I only took my things, nothing of his.

☙ *You must plan this out and do it right; you never want to forget anything and have to turn back. You don't want a reason to have to go back in. And if you have made your final exit and you have left anything behind, remember it is a material item and it can be replaced. No excuses to go back … NONE!*

I had made arrangements how to get to the airport, and everything was set and ready to go.

The evening before, I felt strong and confident. A real sense of relief. I told George I am looking forward to freedom And thanked him over and over again for his friendship.

Now, April 14 has arrived and my big day is here. I left my apartment that morning as if I was going to school the same as I did every day, Monday through Friday. This day was no different from any other. Anus would leave for work by 10:30 AM and get there by 11:00 AM. So, I called him at work to make sure he was there and then the journey started.

My flight was at 1 PM, so I got a ride home from another friend, Martha, who would also take me to the airport. I walked into my apartment and all of a sudden … I froze. Reality hit me and I got SCARED, CRIED, and started to shake; I just couldn't go through with it. I called my mother and told her I wasn't able to do this and I was going to unpack all the boxes before he got home and I wasn't getting on the plane …

I couldn't do this to him … *(Sound familiar?)* I remember he was really nice to me the night before … I remember we had a good night together. Once in a blue moon that would happen. It was like he knew something was up. And I think (no, I know) that was a head trip for me. *(Sound familiar?)*

And with that strong voice of authority, my mother had, she said, "Lyn-Dee, get on that plane!" And that is all I remember hearing.

I took out my list of last minute things I needed to pack, completed the packing, and then I loaded up my friend's truck and grabbed my dog and headed to the airport and got on the plane.

CHAPTER TWO 25

WOW! This was a lot harder then I even thought it would be. Oh my Goodness, and the thoughts that ran through my mind ... how can I, what am I gonna do, how am I gonna, where am I gonna live, what, how, where, why, when? ... All of this were thoughts of fear that were running through my mind. *(Sound familiar?)* But here is what I know, I needed to make a change and the rest would follow because I finally took the first step.

I appreciate my family for being there for me at this time in my life, (blood is thicker than water). But again, they were not the ones that would be able to help me though this and I needed help finding "me."

One moment at a time; one day at a time. So ...

What do you think happened the next morning once Anus found out where I was ... (Oh, you've been here before yourself, huh ... yep, you're right ...)

The phone call came in and the tears that poured out of him! The words, "I am so sorry, I don't deserve you. I will never do it again. You mean the world to me, what was I thinking I will change, I will do anything to get you back, I love you, and I will NEVER EVER DO yata, yata, yata ... TO YOU AGAIN ... I PROMISE...BLA BLA BLA I don't blame you for leaving ... please give me another chance, I promise to ..."
(Sound familiar?)

I told him, I really needed time to pull myself together, please leave me alone to figure this out, but being the type of guy he is, he got on a plane and came to Florida. I was at my girlfriend's house that evening, and he walked in. With tears in his eyes … bla bla bla … he hugged me and I hugged him back. And you know what (and you do), the hug felt demeaning and wrong, but at the same time it felt good to be hugged and loved by him. RIGHT, that damn emotional rollercoaster!

Oh the games, and the thoughts that run through our heads … *he loves me, he is sorry, he seems like he truly means it this time and understands what he was doing to me was wrong and is willing to stop treating me like garbage, I got him where I want him … he is kissing my _____ (this feels good for a change); I have control right now and he will do anything for me … bla bla bla … he is crying and looking in my eyes with sincerity about wanting to change, I think he really means it this time …*

HINT: All those tears are … that flow from their eyes … I've come to realize, is just a fake waterfall of tears, a desperate last resort to get you back . Unfortunately, they work. (*IT'S A TRICK … DON'T FALL FOR IT!*)

And he almost had me, he told me he was going back to Alabama in two days and he wants me to go back with him … So what do you think that made me do? I thought about it, but in the back of my mind, I didn't want to go back, I knew it would have been a mistake, but with that being said, I did consider it …

And then, thank G-D for my friend who told me the next morning … He made a bet with her that I was going back to Alabama with him, "Just watch and see," were his words.

WOW, a BET … I wasn't surprised really, I was … relieved I

guess. I found out and when I did ... I was upset as well, insulted is more like it. I forgot what the bet was, but nevertheless; it was a bet that was a controlling bet. Long story short, he flew back to Alabama alone. Bye-Bye, ANUS!

PART FOUR
The Healing And Finding Out Who Are You?

The second step ... go for counseling. Start by calling the hotlines that are referenced in the back of this book. Who better to speak to than others that have been through what you are going through?

... All it takes is the strength and the desire from the passion in words of wisdom ... that are spoken to you through experience... and you then believe in yourself...for whom you truly are ...

I did call the abuse hotlines and I did go for counseling.

The first question the counselor asked me, (I will never forget it), "Why are you here?" My answer ... "Because I need a third party to hear me, not judge nor give her opinion; I need to vent and release a lot of things before I can get better and the only way to do this is with someone who doesn't know me personally and holds no opinion of anything about my life."

28   TEARS OF FEARS BEHIND CLOSED DOORS

My first visit was a lot of tears and hardcore deep pain being released from inside me. I remember crying like a baby, speaking aloud my feelings and when the first session was over, I felt some kind of relief and finally I had a good night's sleep. I was exhausted.

Now mind you, after each meeting, my mother would always say: *what did you talk about, was it about me, did she say all of your problems are my fault ...* (oh please mom ... stop! This isn't about you). I am sharing this part with you because no one has the right to make you say anything to them you don't want to. That is why you are in counseling!

I would go every week for one hour and it was helping a great deal. I'm learning and getting to know who I am and how wonderful I really am. I felt great about myself and I'm laughing and enjoying life, but this time really enjoying me and life and not just putting on a show for those on the other side of my door.

Now with that being said, please realize that there are still dark moments within myself. No matter what, the insecurities were still inside me as I am sure they are inside you ... would you agree?

Of course, throughout this time, Anus would call me, send me cards and flowers, but I wasn't responding 100 percent. I did talk to him over the phone, (Thank G-D, there weren't such things as cell phones back then).

I would tell him some of my accomplishments and he was very supportive of them. He kept telling me he is changing and loves me, loves me, loves me! He is planning to move back to Florida in four months, would I consider seeing him ... (*Sound familiar?*) (Signs of the trap.) He even said he would go to counseling with me.

The greatest part of my separation from him was getting to know me, the old Lyn-Dee and having fun, or I should say the "NEW Lyn-Dee." Not having to answer to anyone and not having to account to anyone for the seconds in my day; never having to say, "I'm sorry" when it wasn't necessary. WOW! What a great life this is becoming!

Slowly, now when I was looking at my reflection in the mirror, I wasn't spitting at me anymore, I was starting to see a girl who maybe isn't so ugly and maybe isn't so useless ...

Now let me just say, going though this, there were times of joy, and things were much better for me, but it still had its moments of being lonely, scared, insecure. The nights were the worst ... There were nights that were so lonely; I got a big body pillow that was 'woobie.' (And they do work for holding something and wrapping yourself around it. You can find them anywhere today in the bedding department. The one that is really great is the one that they make for pregnant women; go get one)

I would go to sleep so early because I hated the pain of being alone. When I needed a good cry, I would go to the movies and watch a really sad movie just so I could cry and no one would ask me what was wrong or I would cry in the shower.

(*Lyn-Dee-ism*)
You do need to release your emotions, but you need to also

understand, you cannot stay in that emotional place for very long. You are human and you should release your pain, but just don't stay there and have a pity party for yourself.

OK, go to sleep tonight and wake up tomorrow morning feeling the new day. Remember this is the first new day of the rest of your life and it is a blessing.

PART FIVE
Back In Florida – The New Man

Well, the day arrived that Anus was back in town to stay. Yep, he packed up and came back to *save* our marriage. Amazing, he is a Changed Man who knew what he had lost and wanted forgiveness. He learned and understood now and even thanked me for leaving him. It was a major eye opener for him to appreciate what he had.

... Running through my head were my thoughts ... hummm, my marriage or divorce ... try one more time ... my promise to myself ... never get divorced ... so ... I let him back in ... The New Man ...WHY? Because he knows how to treat me and loves me now ... bla bla bla ... (Sound familiar?)

You know, sometimes, depending on who it is coming from, we need to open our eyes and ears to what people are saying to us and again,

CHAPTER TWO

who is saying it to us. Sometimes, those that are looking in, can say what they see, but we, who are going through the nightmare, are in Denial and Hope.

The therapist that counseled me for the past four months, has finally met Anus. Once, twice and then three times. After the third time, he said he didn't need to go anymore and didn't, but he stayed on the nice guy track … *He was everything and more.*

On the fourth visit, which we were supposed to go together, I walked in alone and I will never forget the look on my therapist's face and how hard it was for her to say what she wanted to say to me, but finally she did. Her words, "As a professional, I never say this to my patient, but I have to say it to you … You are too good for your husband … get a divorce." I was shocked, but I knew in the back of my mind, she was right, but again, I didn't listen. Again, I went back into my marriage with the thought, I have to give it one more chance; he is really trying … he was being so great, that he convinced me we were fine and didn't need her anymore. We could spend the money that we were paying her on a nice dinner or go out on date night. And guess what, I stopped going to counseling as well!

Well, I bought into it. He would do anything for me including go to counseling with me, even if it didn't last – he went WOW, what a changed man, great guy. We were happy, laughing, enjoying our married life together. It was perfect and exactly what I've always dreamed my marriage should be.

And slowly, not that I saw the signs yet, things were starting to change back … Very slowly …

We even started our own business, a cleaning business. This was really his puppy to do fulltime; I was just supposed to be the supportive wife. I did keep my full time job during the day. My responsibilities for the business were to do the bookkeeping at night and put together bids for commercial accounts that we got. He was supposed to work the business cleaning. (This was his full time job). We were growing successfully and getting more accounts for residential as well as commercial. We were at the point where we needed to hire one, no more than two employees to help us. And then somehow, all of a sudden, after I worked my day job, I would then come home, cook dinner and change, and go clean the commercial accounts we got. I was exhausted, but would do whatever it took to build our business and help get it off the ground. He didn't want to clean anymore; he wanted to be the boss.

Now, Anus decided that he needed to hire eight more employees when we were not ready for it yet. All he needed to do was to keep cleaning himself and eventually we can add more employees as the new accounts came. But, NO, he didn't want to clean himself anymore and he just wanted to be the BOSS. He wanted to get the jobs done quickly and have a short work day/evening. He didn't want to work the hours it takes to get a business off and running much less put in eight hours a day. He wouldn't listen to me or the accountant, so he hired eight more employees and now we were in the red; we couldn't afford or need the ten fulltime employees, but it didn't matter. He was now back to having a control freak attitude. There wasn't enough money coming in and what happens when you are stressed financially? … You got it …

CHAPTER TWO

I never realized or even saw it coming, here we go again, the trap shut and I was back in the slow process of the invisible abuse.

He was out of control, trying to be in control and of course this led to things getting rocky again between us in just a few short months. Over a matter of time, his true colors were starting to appear again and he was back, but I didn't want to, I guess, admit it was happening again, so ... now I am back to crying and pulling my hair out.

Hating every thought of the moments we would spend together. Looking forward to Monday when I could be at work and dreading the nights and weekends. Damn it ... why is this happening again ... THIS IS JUST WRONG. (*Sound familiar?*)

(Note) ... Please understand and believe, *they just don't change, they wear the nice guy, perfect partner, best friend disguise again and again and again.*

PART SIX
THE CONTROL – WHO AM I?

Now as I go on to tell you my story, realize that the abuse happens to us slowly and it happens to us because we are conditioned not to want to hear them *COMPLAIN* all the time. So when they complain about anything, we make sure to change it so we don't have to hear them ...

What do I mean ... my experience ...

No matter how good you are, you're never good enough. No matter how much you do for them, it is never enough. No matter what ... it is never enough. So, what happens, we get trapped in a world that are *tears of fears behind closed doors*. We will make sure not to do ... or to do ... and we will try so hard to keep the peace that we are now their product of what they can control. We just don't see it as being abused, or maybe we do ... but we don't say it out loud, *why*, because we are so busy trying to what ... keep the peace.

And justify the way we are being treated. Crazy ... but true.

And when there are kids involved, (even if they are not being abused) ... we use the excuse, I don't want to be the reason this family has fallen apart, the kids need their dad. (*Nonsense, na-na, that is no reason to stay. Get over the guilt.*)

We are the peacemakers, but still ... nothing is helping us keep the peace, why, because we do not admit there is abuse happening. We only cry and try ... And the more we try, the worse the abuse gets, it just goes on and on and on and on ...Why? We are doing everything we can to make them happy. But really, once again, it's to 'STOP THEIR COMPLAINING' ... but you know what ... they are just not happy within themselves ... so ... they will complain about anything and everything, no matter what.

Maybe they were controlled; maybe they drink or do drugs that control them. Their job sucks, so they come home and take it

CHAPTER TWO

out on you (and the kids), something twisted their day or night out of whack, so they come home and take it out on you (and the kids). Here is the bottom line ... they are not happy within themselves, they are not happy unless they can control. They are insecure within themselves, but don't admit it. Whatever their excuse is, please understand, it is not your job to be their punching bag, physical or mental. You were not put on this earth to be abused.

♡ STOP BEING TRICKED AND BE STRONGER THEN I WAS ... LEAVE AND STAY AWAY! *They need so much help within themselves to improve themselves and we are not the answer or the solution to helping them through it. Leave that up to the experts to deal with and realize it is not up to you or your responsibility to find that for them either. You need to take charge of your life and only worry about you and your children (if you have any).*

♡ *Please, take a quick break and go to the mirror right now, listen to the songs and look at you, WOW, you are someone so special and now say this to your image and smile.*

> I AM WONDERFUL, I AM SPECIAL, I AM SOMEONE THAT MEANS THE WORLD TO ME AND DAMN IT ... I WILL START CONTROLLING WHAT HAPPENS TO ME! I CAN DO ANYTHING I SET MY MIND TO, ANYTHING! WHY? ... BECAUSE I AM ME ...

Give yourself a kiss, a pat on the back and a hug.

YOU GO GIRL!

PART SEVEN
Having A Baby

Let me fast forward to November 1984. I found out I was pregnant. (I already had a tubal pregnancy when I was 19 and it didn't look as if I can get pregnant again, so when I did, I was *EXCITED, ECSTATIC, THRILLED*). Things were back to how they were in Alabama with us at this point and I truly, strongly, DISLIKED HIM, but now I am pregnant.

I remember coming home from the doctor's office and telling him I was pregnant. His reply was that he didn't want it, how about if he punched me in the stomach or accidentally kicked me in his sleep to make me miscarry. All I know is I told him, he didn't need to be a part of this baby if he didn't want to, but I wasn't going to abort, NO WAY!

Being pregnant should be the happiest time of your life. Looking forward to having a family and planning your future, but that isn't how it was at all for the next several months. I was so happy to be pregnant and loved being pregnant, I just wish I was with someone who could have shared and supported the event, instead, I cried so much when I was pregnant that I truly believed I would have a baby who was depressed. During the next six months, he threw me out more times than I could count, always saying, who would want you now? Back and forth, I played the emotional game of want and desire.

CHAPTER TWO

I was working full time and cleaning at night. I did this all the way through my pregnancy and one week before the baby was born, the doctor said I had to stop working and keep my feet up at all times. I was showing signs of toxemia poisoning and I weighed 200 pounds. When Anus came home and saw me sitting with my feet up, I told him what the doctor said, his response was, 'nonsense,' and he called the doctor and questioned why I had to stop working. Would it be possible for me just to clean at night, we owned a business? Well, the doctor did not give him the answers he wanted and he got mad instead of concerned. He was not happy about the fact that he had to clean. (No need to share with you how pleasant he was from that point on.)

Friends, family, and even others would see what was happening and would even question him about his behavior towards me. But no matter what people would say to him, nothing helped, NOTHING! It just got worse. So now he was back to being a nice guy in front of people, but behind closed doors, he was himself.

Well the evening came when my water broke. We were at a Memorial Day B-B-Q and my good friend, Brett, (may he rest in peace), told me his B-B-Q was gonna cause me to go into labor. At 12:05 AM that night, my water broke. I was lying in bed and called Anus in and the only thing that he could say was, "Get up, you are going to stain the mattress," and then he went and took a shower. While he was in the shower, I called my friend, Rooney to tell her the news and she came right over; she lived in the same complex as we did. He got out of the shower and heard we had company and got very excited.

We get to the hospital and checked in; the nurses put me in a hospital bed in the labor room where I laid there for eight hours, finally only to have a Cesarean section. During the eight hours, he was trying to pick up the nurses, (what an ... *anus* ... the nurses hated him) ... At 8 AM, the doctor ordered a sonogram that determined my baby was breech. At 9:07 AM my daughter, Sica was born. WOW! My reason for living!

She was in the PCICU unit because they said she was having trouble breathing. I didn't see her yet but as soon as I woke up, I asked to see her. She was in the unit upstairs and I asked a nurse to take me to see her; my husband was nowhere to be found. I got to see my daughter for the first time and just held her and rocked her. She was beautiful and ended up to be very healthy. Surprisingly, my daughter was the happiest baby I have ever seen. She was wonderful. How I just loved her, she was my focus and my everything!

PART EIGHT
Bringing The Baby Home & Happily Ever After... Right

We're home after the third day and everything in my house was like a fairy tale family. He was so proud and happy. He was the perfect husband and father. WOW! The past was all worth it, I thought. He was understanding, thoughtful, attentive. Everything that you want in a husband. This is what was missing. A Baby! Now our lives are complete and we can move forward happily.

He absolutely loved his baby girl now that she was here. The look in his eyes when he held her was priceless. She was without any question, his whole world. He truly would do anything for her and *in no way did he do anything that you are about to read, to hurt her intentionally*. He believed that she wouldn't be effected by the abuse that he did to her ... he just knew that this was the only way to get to me. He was such a selfish individual that all he could concentrate on was hurting me and not at all seeing what this was doing to his baby girl.

Three months later. I took the baby to her doctor's appointment and she got a series of shots and did not have a good day at all. (I know you can relate to that if you have had a baby.) All Sica wanted was to be held and rocked, needless to say, nothing was done around the house that day and dinner was not ready/nor made when he got home. Thinking he would understand and help when he got home; maybe he would hold Sica so I could at least get some things done. WRONG! I never expected the *old ANUS* to walk into the house at six-ish and scream ... "Where the hell is dinner, what did you do all day, sit on your ass? What about me and my needs? Damn it, what good are you?" I just looked at him with amazement. OH NO ... HE'S BACK!

With that, I tried to explain, but there wasn't any excuse that was good enough for him ... Get this ... he threw me and the baby out. That's right, I had to pick up our stuff that he *threw outside* and load up my van with my baby in one arm and move back to my mother's that night.

(Now keep in mind that I would help with the business, cleaning our commercial accounts at night when I could. I would have my mother-in-law, (who was the sweetest women you've ever met), watch Sica for a few hours).

The next day ... the phone call, the visit and the tears. Anus cried, "I don't know what I was thinking, I just had a really rough day." ... bla, bla, bla ... (*Sound familiar?*) Not to drag this out for you ... I went back. Thinking to myself because of what others were saying ... 'You have a baby, you need to try to work this out.' They would tell me they spoke to him, he is so sorry and I think he really means it. Give him another chance. OK ... here I go again!

Chance after chance after chance. This happened three more times.

And, it didn't take long nor did it last long each time for him to turn back into himself ... it happened a few more times that he threw us out when my daughter was between the ages of three months and fifteen months. "This is just wrong," I thought to myself. But I kept going back because, "How can I not try to make us a better family?" The baby needs her father ... (*Sound familiar?*)

Towards the end of this marriage nightmare, get this one ... when he would get angry at me ... he realized he couldn't say or do anything to me anymore and get a response ... it just didn't faze me. I was now at the point where I would just ignore him. I was 100% focused on my baby. So, what did he do when he couldn't get a reaction from me? Go through my child.

CHAPTER TWO 41

Guess what ... it worked, he got my attention again! Don't mess with a mother's child.

Again, he was in no way trying to harm his daughter emotionally. He was using her to get to me. He never thought unfortunately that what he was doing to her mentally was harming her and eventually, would destroy his relationship with her. His main focus was to get to me. How sad, but true, that he never realized what he was doing. I call that a very sick man. (*Does this sound familiar?*)

The rollercoaster ride is almost over. Anus I am done with you and your attitude.

PART NINE
The Final Straw

The evening the straw broke the camel's back ...

My baby girl, Sica, was fifteen months old, playing on the living room floor. Happy, laughing, and watching Sesame Street. I was getting dinner ready and he came home early. I said, "Hi Daddy, you're home early." He just went off. Yelling, acting like an idiot! I ignored him ... I just looked at him, turned off the oven, and stopped cooking ... I then said to him ... "I am DONE!"

That evening, it was time to give Sica her bath ... Where's her soap? Where's her shampoo? Where is her ...? Now, I have to ask you ... is this normal? This all started happening when I was to the point of, *This is it*, ENOUGH! *I AM DONE AND IT IS OVER!*

Now, to get my attention and show me who's boss ... he would take all the baby's things, (I had to use special soap for Sica for her sensitive skin, shampoos, vitamins and of course her food, etc.). HE WOULD TAKE EVERYTHING AND HIDE THEM!

As I was looking for everything, he put it back and said I was going crazy, they were there all the time. After I used them, he hid them again.

The next morning ...

At 9 AM, *you bet your life*, I was on the phone with an attorney and by 10:00 AM that morning, I was at the attorney's office filing for my divorce.

The Question of the Day ... Are you sure? YES! The attorney warned me that the judge is going to insist we go for mediation before he'd give me the divorce ... I said we have already tried that ... It is time for the DIVORCE without any obstacles in the way.

Because we owned a condo together, I could not move out or I would have given up my rights to ownership and would have lost at that time what was a lot of money to me. Since I paid the mortgage and the bills as well for the past several years, I needed what was my share. Until the divorce was finalized, only three

CHAPTER TWO

weeks away, we had to live together. (Of course, he would treat me nicely because he wanted me to stop the divorce ... BUT NOT THIS TIME ANUS, BYE-BYE ANUS FOR GOOD!

OH, I was so excited that I was going through with my divorce. I had peace of mind that I knew I did everything I could to save my marriage. I accepted that the divorce wasn't my fault, and I didn't fail. It wasn't my failure, so I now could move on with my life.

No matter what, I was smiling and not crying at all. When he came home, I was pleasant and I didn't let anything bother me, none of his words, his actions, nothing. I had everything under control, from me to the caring of Sica and her needs, I just let go of every feeling I had about my marriage ... But now with the mindset that I would NEVER marry again LOL!

During the wait for the divorce, I didn't trust Anus, no matter how nice and helpful he tried to be. I would keep everything for Sica at my mother's house and every evening, I would go there with Sica, bath her there, eat dinner there and pack up whatever I needed for her the next day and hide it. Isn't that ridiculous? Yep, I did that ... I had a cooler for anything that needed to be kept cold. Now I ask you, is this any way to live and raise your child? Are you relating to this, *does it sound familiar?*

STOP THE INSANITY. It is time to change things in your life and for your life.

Here is what I will share with you ... when you have had enough and your feelings are DEAD inside for your partner ... it is over and nothing can change it. NOTHING. We, as women, put up with A LOT ... but when it's over ... it's over.

🙾 *Pick and choose who to listen to. Never believe or listen to anyone that will defend your partner, listen to yourself and others that have been where you are. You are the one living in hell, not them. They are clueless to what is going on behind closed doors. Outsiders saying, children need both parents, stay married for the children ... Here's what I have to say about that ... GARBAGE! ABSOLUTELY NOT! Get out. The house is not a happy place for anyone ... your kids hear and feel everything that is going on and they now have their own emotions to deal with because of it. Save yourself and your kids. As they get older, they will understand. They may not understand as it is happening, but remember, you are the parent, you do know what is best. The kids might be angry, but they will understand one day. Please, make sure you reassure the child(ren) that under no circumstance is it their fault.*

Keep in your mind; you are changing your lifestyle for them and for you to have a brighter future ... and there is a brighter future just waiting for you to take the first step through the door of "Your New Beginning."

CHAPTER 3

PART ONE

*F*ree & *S*ingle *P*arenting

"*D*" DAY HAS ARRIVED. Let's start this chapter off on a positive note!

Good news ...
#1 – I got my divorce
#2 – The judge made the ruling for him to move out until we sold the condo or he bought me out and then I would move out and he could move back in. No problem there. (This was the only thing the judge did in my favor and granting me $300 a month child support.)

HURRAY! Sept. 24, 1986, wake up, feeling good about the day

and arrived in court at 9:00 AM. I am getting my divorce and I was happy ☺. I even told my boss at the time, I'll be in after court. I'll be single, and I'll be free of him … so I thought …

The Judge was a Man's Judge and a real piece of work (Negative term).

The judge was a royal jerk to put it mildly. He was 100% for the men and made it perfectly clear to me that if I did anything to stand in the way of the father/daughter relationship, I would be in contempt, and I could go to jail. Well, that wasn't a problem, I had no intentions of taking my daughter away from her father and he gave Anus his visitation rights. No problem, he had her every other weekend.

With that being said, the judge said quite a few off the wall things that just destroyed me. I couldn't even go back to work that day.

Once again, since we are divorced now, there was nothing he could do to me or say to me that would affect me. He knew that and now would use Sica as the weapon even more than ever.

PART TWO
BEING A DIVORCED PARENT, DEALING WITH AN ABUSIVE MAN …

Please understand I will not disclose everything that he had

CHAPTER THREE

done to Sica to get through to me, in respect to her and also to protect my daughter's privacy. I will share with you ... it was another nightmare for the next eleven years of trying to keep Sica safe and at the same time for me not to end up in jail.

I will not be going into great details of the abuse Sica has experienced; I don't feel that is necessary, we all understand what abuse is, being beaten down mentally and physically, to the extreme of losing your own identity.

If at all possible, never take away your child(ren)'s family from his side. If you can ... IF his family is as wonderful as Anus's was. I know there are many families that are impossible to deal with, they will defend your abuser no matter what ... if that is the case ... don't worry, forget about it! You have enough to deal with. But just food for thought, if they are nice and kind ... then ...

One of ways I thought would help me protect Sica was to reach out to his family ... and they were wonderful, they were not in denial of who Anus was. However, even they could only do so much. I also made sure that under no circumstances would Sica NOT know his side of the family because they were wonderful ... it was him that was the bad seed. I made sure that Sica would see her grandparents often and her other relatives on his side. Mind you, there were some family members that didn't care too much for me after the divorce, but they were able to put their feelings aside and love Sica. I told them, "Things just didn't work out in my marriage," (I never belittled Anus to his family and yes that was hard, but I never said anything nice about him either ... catch my drift ...) "but we do have Sica and Sica needs to know you. You don't have to hang out with me at all, all you have to do is call me and I can drop Sica off to spend some time with you and then I will pick her up. If you want to spend an hour with her, fine, a day, fine ... as long as she gets to see you."

🕉 *Remember what I said earlier about my Uncle? Your child(ren) need positive, good people in their lives. If there are good people that can be a part of their lives, let them be a part of their lives. You don't have to agree with everything or everyone ... as long as it's not a traumatic problem ... then deal with the child(ren) getting well rounded and having positive people in their lives.*

You need to speak to his family members, like I did and just make them realize, if at all possible, that it isn't about anyone else but the child(ren), and ask them, "Can we get along for the kids and leave out the problems I have with the ex?"

Again, I know this doesn't and can't work with all families, after all, blood is thicker than water ... but the child(ren) are their blood, hopefully they will see that and put aside whatever feelings they have towards you. Hopefully, you'll have their support and be able to have this kind of a relationship with his side that I had with mine ... if not, it is their loss and at least you tried. Don't beat yourself up over it ... As long as you tried ... forget them if it can't happen. Remember, you didn't fail, you did everything you could to make a positive impact for your child(ren).

ANUS, ANUS, ANUS ... I had no choice but to take Anus back to court, (trust me, I wasn't going back in front of this judge unless it was absolutely necessary) and only a couple of times with proof of things that he was doing to and with Sica. Because I was broke and couldn't afford the justice my daughter needed

CHAPTER THREE

… I would have to go in front of the same judge … my thoughts were, because of the proof I had, there would be no way the judge wouldn't see what was happening and he would help *protect* Sica. (So, I thought …).

Wrong again Lyn-Dee … the judge not only sided with Anus, but now also gave him more time with Sica.

There was a time when Sica was 5 years old that I had to get the State Health & Human Service Agency involved to protect her and they did help; they suspended his visitation rights for a short period of time.

It was crazy when this happened. He knew his rights were taken away, he got the call from the state to stay away from us and what does he do … he called the police on me. He said my daughter was being abused by me and get this … *she was being hung in a closet!*

When I saw the police outside my apartment, I had Sica go into my bedroom and watch one of her movies. I closed the door so she wouldn't hear what was going on.

The police knocked on my door with Anus. I opened it and saw two cops looking very concerned and authoritative. I told the police they can come in but needed to leave him outside please; I would explain once they were inside, and they did. I had them call the state to verify the information I was telling them was true and it was. They looked through my apartment only to find a wonderful child's bedroom, a clean home, and a happy, clean child who was not being abused. They apologized and left, going down stairs and yelling at Anus that he is in violation and if he ever pulled this again, they would arrest him. Thank G-D the police listened and understood!

Just so you understand, the abuse that was going on with Sica, she didn't feel as if her daddy didn't love her … (most kids don't), he wasn't mean to her per se, she was always clean and taken care of on the outside. But the cheap jerk would swap her clothes. I would send her with clothes that fit her and he would send her back with clothes that were too small and keep the newer clothes. He said, "I give you child support." *(Bet you've heard that one before if you are divorced or separated)*. It is what happened behind closed doors that nobody can see or hear.

It was as if the things he did were hidden from her, yet happening to her but were meant for me (mental abuse, physical abuse). Inappropriate things she would watch that he would rent for her at the video store, the gun she was learning to use even after the law was passed that guns and all fire arms should be stored in a locked box up high, out of sight and out of the reach of a child. (He sent her home with a picture, showing me … my daughter and the gun.) Places he would take her that you wouldn't take a child. All sorts of things that were allowed, but shouldn't have been.

We even had to go to parenting mediation, court ordered, and the counselor there asked him, why would you do these things? She is so young? But did he stop? Nope!

There is an article about this judge saying the same things to another lady when she was going through her divorce that he said to me. How this judge was a judge is beyond me.

CHAPTER THREE

In the world we live in, to be able to have access to the justice system for attorneys, we all understand it is costly and if you don't have the green, it can be very frustrating and I felt as if the system was against me. I didn't have the green, so to say the least, I felt helpless. There is a solution for this problem at the end of this book.

Every time Sica came home, how she would speak to me, even in her young age voice with a limited vocabulary ... what she would say or do and how she would respond to me ... things she would do while playing with her little friends ... all the signs of abuse were right there. When I did go in front of the judge with *proof*, I was threatened that I was the one going to jail if I said one more word or tears would roll down my face. HOW IS THAT? (Not all judges are good.) I wanted to say so much, but when you are warned ... "One more word out of your mouth young lady and you are going to jail!" You think real quick, if I am in jail, I cannot protect her. You need to be there for her so ... SHUT UP and deal with it to the best of your ability and control yourself, so I did.

Your kids come home from their father's and tell you, you are bad, you are mean, you don't do anything, it is all your fault that daddy is not here ... "I want _____. Daddy said he gives you money so you have to buy it for me ..."

And when the children come back home to you after spending a short amount of time with their father, (who they think is FANTASTIC because they get to stay up late, do things they normally can't when they are with you ...) now, you have to re-mold the kids back to normal behavior, (which usually takes a few days, right) only to turn them back over to their father again. Visit after visit ... you are the mean parent, you are a bad mommy ...

There were so many things happening to Sica as the years went on mentally, that I couldn't stop. The only thing I could do was to be there to support and love her and pray that the day will come when she will see the light.

(On a side note ... I totally understand how some mothers hide their children from the abusive parent and go to jail because they will not say where the child (ren) is/are.) My hat is off to them. (please understand, I am not saying this course of action should be done, I am just saying, I understand.)

With all that was happening and going on, I still would not say anything bad about Anus to her or about him in front of her. (Here is where I changed his name to ANUS so she never knew who I was talking about). I knew if I spoke badly about him, it would come back to haunt me, I also knew if I didn't say anything bad about him to her, eventually ... down the road ... she would see him for who he is and she would make up her own mind. And she did 11 years later... but she did.

Same story, different faces and names ... It would take me three to four days to get her back on track, only for it to happen again and again. Are you relating to this? (*Sound familiar?*)

On his weekends, I very rarely slept and had a hard time having a good time with friends, knowing he was planning how to get to me through my daughter.

CHAPTER THREE

The judge was useless to Sica and I. Anus had the green therefore the justice system was challenging for me ... just keep praying ... (back then, if you didn't have the green $$$ ... you couldn't have the justice.) Again, there is a solution for you to have access to the justice system way more then I did. Information in the back of the book.

It took 11 years before this nightmare was over when Sica finally said ... "Enough Mommy, I don't want to go to daddy's anymore."

*Na, Na ... don't allow
anything or anyone to
keep you on a
path of hopeless
dreams and undeliverable
promises!*

*isn't it time to create
your new path ...
look up and outside the window
and follow your dreams.*

☺

~~Woobie~~

CHAPTER 4

PART ONE

Sica Had Enough ...

It was Christmas morning, 1996 at 10:30 AM; she called me crying from her grandmother's house phone and told me, "Daddy kicked me out of the house and I am not allowed back in, please come and get me." And when I arrived, she was sitting on the curb ... crying. She got in, we drove away, and when we were out of sight, I pulled over and gave her a hug and kiss. She made me promise that she wouldn't have to go back to him again ... and she didn't ... HER CHOICE!

And that was the day, we finally had peace ... she never want back. Our lives were now peaceful and on the right track. However, the scars inside her were there and this is something we still have to deal with to this day.

Anus had the nerve to call me and tell me I should talk to Sica and make her go back to him, I should ground her for her behavior and insist that she apologize to him. I laughed and just hung up the phone. Why bother even trying to talk to him, it wasn't worth it.

The beauty of the phone … you can hang UP! LOL. And that was the end of the relationship with him and her.

(Don't worry … as long as you don't belittle their father EVER, the kids will see through it. It can take years … but the truth will come out in the long run. As they say, 'Time will either expose you or promote you.')

Just stay strong, I know it is hard … but stay strong and just always be there for the children.

Yes, Sica went for counseling, however, eleven years of abuse just doesn't go away … ever … just because you seek help. It only teaches us how to deal with it and be stronger for it.

PART TWO
Over The Rainbow – During The 20 Years After The Divorce

And this is when I started the Personal Development

CHAPTER FOUR

Life was a lot better than it was, no doubt … there were some bumps in the road … but I will take these bumps over the other bumps any day.

Were there times that I would cry because I was alone, *yes*.

Were there times I couldn't afford food, *yes*.

Were there times when I felt insecure, lonely, and depressed, *yes*.

Were there times that I didn't understand the emotional rollercoaster I was going through, happy, sad, crying, and even mad for no reason, *yes*.

Do I still feel them every now and then … *yes*.

Was I ever scared … *yes*, but not the way I was before.

No matter how hard the times got, and they did get hard, I never regretted leaving my past and getting my divorce.

In many ways, it was exciting to see what I can and have accomplished on my own … what I learned and how I was able to do so many things. I became very diversified. If there was an opportunity and they were willing to train with no experience and it intrigued me, I applied.

And you know what? They were all good times in their own rights.

Now understand and believe, I was not good at everything I tried, some things I was just really bad at, but you know what? At least I tried and I learned from everything I did, whether I succeeded or failed at it ... I learned a lesson from everything and everything I did taught me how to do things differently and/or better.

In the beginning of the book, I spoke about personal development because it is important for you to fit this in your life for the rest of your life. One of the biggest things I get out of personal development is ... failing my way to success in every avenue of life. And you can and will do the same. Sometimes it is frustrating ... but then it is rewarding.

I was failing my way to the top. I just didn't know where the top would be. LOL! I was just so happy and proud of myself for trying and giving it 110% that that was good enough for me. I knew it would not be the end ... it was just another learning curve on my journey to my future. I did not beat myself up over my failures ... NO ... I learned from them and so will you. Never give up, failure is not an option; it is only another learning curve. Again ... failure is not an option ... it is only another learning curve! Never Give UP!

In order for you to be successful in anything, you must fail first to become great at it. Example, when you first started to ride a two-wheeler bike, how many times did you fall? A LOT And then finally, you were riding. (OK ... you can't ride a bike ... lol ... another example ... think of something you were bad at in the beginning and now it is second nature to you, could be cooking, cleaning, whatever ... see ... you failed your way to success.) And you will do it again and again and again. That is how you are going to allow the greatness within you to shine, SHINE, SHINE!

CHAPTER FOUR

PART THREE
New Relationships

After my divorce, about 4 months later, I met a nice guy, and I was with him for 5 years. I still was not going to ever get married again. Great guy, and thank G-D for the modern-day times; living with someone was OK to do. So, why would I ever get married?

In my heart, no matter how nice this guy was, he wasn't even close to me entering the idea of marriage. I remember he would bring up the subject of marriage and I pretty much treated the topic as a deaf ear.

I injured my back in 1987 at work, (four **herniated disks later**, L-1 to L-5). Wow, this was tough, but we survived. My boyfriend moved in with Sica and me so he could be there for us and help. Made extra money working from home, doing the bookkeeping for two businesses. Even though I was bedridden, I was able to make calls from my house to sell bags and flags for the veterans. I was admitted into a rehab hospital for two weeks and then had a lot of physical therapy for the next few years to come. With the help of my boyfriend and my parents, we made it through. (My boyfriend was great with my daughter and me, very supportive, helping me with Sica who was two years old, and dealing with Anus.)

Financially, I was scrapping the bottom of the peanut butter jar. As long as I had food on the table for Sica, I didn't care if I ate cheap crackers every day. My parents did help when they saw our refrigerator was empty.

During that time I also got pregnant, it was another tubal pregnancy. OK, got through that one. One year later to the day, another tubal pregnancy. Got through that one too. That made four pregnancies and only one was good. Thank G-D for my baby girl who I loved before I even saw her, my Sica.

As time went on, I also dappled into a few business ventures, credit recovery; also created, sewed and sold costumes; and worked doing telemarketing and other things, always keeping the door of opportunity open.

Then after five years of being in a relationship, we split and we went our separate ways as friends. I then decided to be alone with my daughter for a year and a half. This was the best thing I could have done for myself. I not only ventured into many different areas of producing an income, I was learning I could do anything. I may have not made a lot of money and I was just getting by, but you know what, whatever I had, it was mine and whatever I did, I was proud of it. I was able to support Sica and me, living in a nice area, in a nice apartment.

Looked into some MLM's (Multi Level Marketing businesses from home) and got involved in some … I would be open to really anything that I can make money at home with, (that was legal … LOL). Made some money, lost some money, but gained a lot of knowledge along the way. Mind you, not having the lifestyle of the rich and famous, just the life style of the proud and sane. LOL. Having fun and sleeping at night.

CHAPTER 5

PART ONE
After Getting To Know Me

After a year and a half, I met another guy who I was with for almost twelve years ... again, never wanting to get married. I refused to settle and I just didn't see it in the future. I know you are thinking, My Gosh, Lyn-Dee, it was twelve years ... LOL ... I know. This guy was so nice in so many ways, he was wonderful to my daughter and me ... but the only reason I was with him for so long to be honest with you, is #1, I felt sorry for him. He had no family, and lived a very quiet life. Didn't have much ambition to do new things, he was a bit of a complainer, negative attitude, (you can look at the glass, and say it is half-empty or half-full). However, he was thoughtful and caring; he was a great friend to Sica and me. And great friends are hard to find. Moreover, I didn't believe that love existed in the world and I really didn't care about a relationship. As a matter of fact, we were more friends than anything else.

With that being said, it did get to the point where it was draining and life is too short to try to make someone else happy that just doesn't see the brighter side of life. I was also totally outgrowing this so called relationship. So this too had to end and it did, once again, still friends to this day.

PART TWO
CAREER

During that relationship, I got very wrapped up in work and now owned two businesses. A hair salon, (that I really owned to help a friend out) and a pet store that I owned for the guy I was with for twelve years. Loved both industries and became a workaholic. Now I am running crazy every day, 7 days a week, 16 hours a day for two businesses and being a mom. WOW!

It is true, you can do anything. You can become someone and do whatever it takes. However, there is always a price to pay ... good, bad or indifferent. We get to pick and choose. Remember, in life there is always a choice. Some you think you will regret,

CHAPTER FIVE

others you will be proud of ... no matter what, they are all lessons we learn from.

Problem with being so busy while your children are minors ...

Now that I had two full time businesses, (which I promised myself, I would *never* even own one business as long as Sica was a minor ... let alone two ... knowing how much your children need you to be home with them). I thought I was and would always be there for her and could do it all. I thought owning my own business would also give me more flexibility, when in fact, that was just an illusion. Owning your own businesses, especially at the beginning, robs you of all your time. Who knew? Times 2 no less. I was blinded by my daughter's independence and thinking I was there for her, when in fact again, now looking back, I was always in a hurry and not paying attention to everything that was going on with her. I do regret this more then I can ever express. I am so sorry Sica.

When there were emergencies, yes, I would drop everything and run, but again ... maybe if I wasn't so busy, they wouldn't have happened ... but ... *I can't beat myself up over it, but I do regret this and always will ...*

It was the summer that Sica was at the end of eight grade, going into ninth, high school, when I started the businesses. Now she was starting to have boyfriends, not many, but not the best choice of guys either. (I believe this is where I spoke earlier in the book, Chapter 2, of how the children would respond to a guy giving them a nice smile and hug). We as parents can only give our opinion and pray. We cannot be there with them 24/7.

But again, I regret not being there for her to watch all the signs of her relationships. But then again, all kids are good in front of you, so would these things have happened anyway ... don't know, but probably.

> *Parents can only give good advice or put them (children) on the right paths, but the final forming of a persons' character lies in their own hands.*
>
> *~Anne Frank~*

Before I knew it, four years flew by and I was sitting at her high school graduation. At the beginning of her high school life, she was doing great, or so I thought. Throughout her high school years, she maintained good grades, was involved with the ROTC program at school, and loved it. Everything seemed to be fine. Then when she was a senior, all hell broke loose. Still getting good grades ... but now in love with a guy that was older and out of school.

PART THREE
Kids Now Dating ...

A man who was eight years older than her. (Accepting the love from an older guy ... maybe deep down as a father figure ... *just a thought, what do you think?*)

Of course, my first reaction was to talk to this guy and I asked

CHAPTER FIVE

him point blank … "What does a 25-year-old guy, want with a 17-year-old girl?" He said, "She is special and mature." He said he really cared for her like no other.

Yes, I told him what I thought and my feelings. I asked him not to see her; he was too old for her. They respected my wishes, but then after a few months, Sica wanted to see him, she was honest with me and at that point, I could either accept it or they would just go behind my back. I accepted it.

We would have dinner together occasionally and he seemed nice and caring to her. Long story short, she was 'in-love' with him, now she wanted to move in with him. 'My 17-year-old daughter who knew it all.'

Before, she moved out, I thought she wouldn't be able to by law, because she was a minor and still in school. I called up an attorney through Pre-Paid Legal to confirm my belief in what the law is and I was WRONG. At the age of 16, if she wanted to, she could move out and there wasn't a damn thing I can do about it. Isn't this crazy? Minors can't vote, can't drink, can't apply for any credit, but they can move out. She knew it too, so she moved out. *(Find out what the age is in your state.)*

Then the signs were starting to appear, but by this time … she wasn't opening up to me … I was so busy, and because she wasn't living in my house anymore, I really didn't see any of the abuse that was happening to her. She would wear lightweight long sleeve shirts, pants and I never gave it a second thought. Maybe the classrooms were cold via A/C … I didn't pay attention to this sign. But then again, all the kids dressed like this.

The worst day of my parenting life came when I got a call for help from her at 1 PM in the afternoon. YES I DROPPED EVERYTHING AND RAN TO HER! Only to learn of the nightmare she was going through that started since she was in the eighth grade.

In this relationship with this 25-year-old guy, she was beaten down so badly mentally and physically, that we were now in the mental ward of a hospital for eight hours, everything was taken away from her while she was in there, all her personal belongings. We just talked to each other, she was opening up to me, we were crying, laughing, but hurting deeply inside. (I am so, so sorry Sica). But still, she didn't tell me everything, I found out more that evening ...

In the mean time, while we were in the hospital, I stepped out and put a call into her boyfriend and told him if he ever came near her again, @#$%^$#@@#$. I requested him not to call her or try to see her, if he did ... @#$%^&*(*&^%$#.

When we got home that evening (back to my house), she was settling into her room. Her friend came over and took me outside and told me more, she feared for Sica's life, he was going to kill her. She never came to me before because Sica told her not to, (as a friend, she did what was asked, she wanted to have Sica's trust and for Sica to be able to go to her), but it got to this point where her friend had to spill the beans. (Now mind you, Sica did tell me of some of the abuse, but not all of it).

Her friend really had a hard time confiding in me, I told her ... I knew something was seriously wrong now, more than what Sica

CHAPTER FIVE

told me that day. I told her friend, "Sica is going to be mad at you for telling me whatever it is that you need to tell me, (I could feel at this point, what she wanted to tell me). She is going to be mad at you and probably not talk to you for awhile, I promise you this, she will come around eventually, here is your choice ... you can tell me and help save her life or not tell me and end up at her funeral." She started to cry and totally opened up to me and told me things Sica didn't throughout the day.

Advice ...
(If you know this is happening to someone you care about ... go the distance and reach out to the family that can help ... your friend will be mad and angry ... but one day they will come back to you.)

I was beside myself ... all I saw was the color red! Her phone was going crazy with calls from him. I finally got the phone from her and answered it, his reply ... she keeps trying to call me, she has been calling me all day. Needless to say ... that was impossible, in the hospital, she wasn't allowed to have her phone; they took it. HE LIED and LIED TO ME. NOT GOOD! I called the police and asked them to meet me at his home and what had been going on. (I was calling the police so I didn't end up in jail). I did need to confront him and have him look into my eyes so he got my message loud and clear. He had left his house by the time we arrived, (within fifteen minutes). The police were now looking for him because he was driving with a suspended license. He was slick and they did not find him. I did finally speak to him and told him ... @#$%^# STAY AWAY FROM MY DAUGHTER!

Like most abused people, Sica was ready to accept his apology and did ... but every time I heard his name or thought she was with him ... I spoke to her and spoke to him ... the relationship did finally end ... but it took awhile.

During this chapter of Sica's learning curve of life, I learned everything from her becoming a cutter in the eighth grade and hating herself. We did get through it and that will be a story that maybe one day, Sica will share with you. I am very happy to say, we, she survived it all and is now a wonderful mother of a beautiful baby girl, Briana. (Not with the guy above).

However, her wounds are deep and the scars are there, and they still appear every now and then. We both are there for each other and we are today best friends through thick and thin. We both know we can and do count on one another.

The reason I shared that with you, is so maybe you will learn from my experience, my mistakes that no career opportunity is worth the time your children need you the most, please don't make the same mistake I did. I am sharing this with you, why ... not to tell you about my daughter's nightmare, but to share with you that just maybe what I said in Chapter 2, and I repeat below ... has a valid point.

If your child(ren) is/are the product of an abusive father or a father that had disappeared out of their lives, please be aware of the signs of low self-esteem and having no confidence within themselves. Get them professional help, suggest they call a hotline whenever they need to vent and as they are growing-up, try to help them the best you can. It is hard sometimes to see the signs, just be there for them and support them through their

CHAPTER FIVE

hard times. Especially when they are teenagers and know it all. (Life is not easy for them or you.)

You can never turn back the hands of time ... you can only learn from how you spend it and grow.

PART FOUR
Sharing Some Other Nightmares

I have known people that were/are beaten up so badly and were/are sexually abused, (raped) by their boyfriend/husbands/partners, over and over again ... It is sad and very scary. We're all crying together and blame ourselves for how we were/are being treated by our partner...or we justify why this is happening to us. The funny thing is we will tell each other to get out of the relationship ... but none of us did/do ... until we are ready.

I know women that scar themselves by digging into their skin with their own nails and leaving outer scars to release their pain from within. I know women who will drink themselves to sleep, take pills, only to wish they never woke up the next morning. Bottom line, we can all survive the abuse as long as we have support. Please realize you have Support.

I have met so many people, young and old, all different walks of life that you would never imagine have been abused or are abused. I know the most successful businesswomen who are abused and you would never know it and I know of housewives that are abused and you would never know it. I know women whose spouses are professional entrepreneurs, lawyers, doctors, police officers, all the way down to jobless wonders. All walks of life. Sometimes you will never know of all the women that have low self-esteem, lack of self-worth, and lack of self-respect all because of the abuse they encounter. Being humiliated and degraded but holding their heads up high outside their doors of tears of fears.

There are so many men who come across as a prince only to really be horrible, abusive men. Are you living with one? Are you like I was, hiding your tears of fear on the outside and showing everyone that life is good and there aren't any problems at home? Or are you having a hard time hiding the abuse and people are telling you to get out, but you can't see that happening and now they are telling you stop complaining about it if you are not going to do something about it?

Whichever you are, I understand. Nothing is easy when it comes to the final closure, so please don't beat yourself up over it, but do get help and start walking toward the light of freedom.

… If anyone ever says to you that you are a volunteer victim, (what do I mean by that, people are saying to you, you keep staying with your partner, you aren't willing to do anything about it, so stop complaining …) Just understand they have never been through any kind of abuse and they just don't get it. With that being said, there is some truth to what they are saying … they just don't get the part, where it isn't easy getting out. Of course it is possible, very

CHAPTER FIVE 71

do-able, but the right way ... just not easy!

As the time went on in Alabama, I thought I was going crazy. And it got to the point where I would absolutely dread the weekends. Home for 48 hours with him. How many hours are you spending with your "Anus" and dreading it?

Take action and ...
Call your local/state abuse hotline and just start talking to others who are there to help you. You need to start venting and let it out. Talk to others that have been where you are and will not be judging you at all. You can find the contact information to your abuse center in your state in the back of this book. You don't even have to go find it, it is already in your hands. PLEASE ... JUST CALL!

Just a few of many true stories that maybe you can relate to:

STORY #1

(This is a very close friend of mine who was going through abuse at the same time I was going through mine. We spent countless hours together trying to support each other emotionally. That is why this one story is longer than the others ...)

I will never forget this as long as I live ... it was Christmas Eve and a few friends were all supposed to get together. It was one of those evening's were we would all bring something, (potluck). I remember I needed something for my dish and I went over to my friend's house and her boyfriend answered the door and told me she wasn't able to come to the door, she was in the shower. (You know that feeling you get when something's just not right

… yeah, I felt it). My girlfriend never showed up with her boyfriend, he showed up alone and said my friend wasn't feeling well … Well, I of course went to her house, only to find her badly beaten up, her ribs were broken, (all of them) and she couldn't move. This wasn't the first time I have seen this happen to her, but it was the worst. As a friend, you are there to support and love her and do whatever she asked you to do, which was always, "Please don't say anything to him or anyone for that matter, please. It was my fault …"

I gave her a big hug and just held her for a long time … crying together. She told me that when I knocked on the door before, I stopped him from hitting her more. I interrupted his beating and he raped her. Again, crying to me, "Please don't say anything to him." And of course I did as she asked, but I could not look at him nor speak to him when I went back to the get together … He knew I knew, I just couldn't say anything in fear that he would go back to her and beat her again.

As a friend, you do what is requested so your friend always has a place to turn to … I knew that the beatings were going to get worse … I knew that he would *kill* her … I told my best friend … enough now, it has to be over … he is going to *kill* you … with tears in her eyes and shaking like a leaf as if it was a cold winter night, she was so scared, not knowing what to do or how to do it. Justifying again the beatings and the rapes. It was time to do something to save her life … and I do mean that … SAVE her life!

There was another friend of ours who I spoke to about the situation, (who also knew about the abuse) and we both agreed, this

CHAPTER FIVE 73

just can't go on any longer, he will kill her. So with that, we decided to go to her father and tell him his daughter is being badly abused and she needs help. You see, I understand ... we, (the abused) will forgive the abuser, we will accept their apologizes and keep living the lie of happiness ...

I knew my friend would be livid at me, I knew she would be so angry, she wouldn't speak to me for awhile. I knew she was going to hate me ... but I also knew the only way to get this creep out of her life was to get her father involved at this point, who would make sure his daughter is safe and the abusive jerk was OUT!

And to make a long story short, she was mad at me, just like I said she would be. But her father got her abuser out of her house and after a period of time, out of her life. Yes, she still saw him, but the relationship was fading and then finally ended. And what happened to her, she found an incredible man who loves her and is truly her best friend today.

STORY #2

A friend of mine is married to a cop. This couple on the outside is the perfect couple, but behind closed doors are tears of fears. He beat her so badly that it was painful to be around them if you knew what was truly going on. She would not do or say anything about it because she said he would lose his job. Now he is retired and a very, very sick man, only to have her take care of him. He is too weak to beat her now, but now she has to be his nurse. What about her life? This is one of those, 'Why didn't I leave so I could have a life?' Now she would feel guilty to even think about leaving him because of his health challenges, she will not leave him because she has a big heart. To this special survivor, my dear friend ... I am always here for you.

STORY #3

A friend of mine loses her two children because the man who so violently abused her, now killed her children to get back at her, really his intentions where for her to see her children dead and then to kill her, when in fact, he ended up killing himself because the cops came. Very sad. *(See newspaper article below)*

Sun-Sentinel

November 28, 2004   Fort Lauderdale, FL

Distressing Tale of Abuse; Broward Agency Helps Plantation Woman Get Her Life Back on Track after Tragedy

By Karla D. Shores, Education Writer

She was an executive assistant at Motorola in Sunrise, where her husband of nearly 14 years worked as an engineer.

He was in a men's service group and she worked in the nursery at a church in Plantation. They lived comfortably with their two young children in a four-bedroom house in Plantation.

But Nancy Horneman, 46, who suffered through a turbulent marriage and lost her two children to domestic violence, tells her story as if her life began more than five years ago, on Jan. 1, 1999, when, after she suffered a particularly brutal beating, police showed up at her house.

Her bruises were still fresh. Her lip was split and her body ached from being thrown through two rooms.

The officer handed Horneman a business card and told her,

CHAPTER FIVE

"You don't deserve this. It will only get worse. There are people who will help you," she recalled.

The card listed contact numbers for a place Horneman knew nothing about – Women In Distress. But the organization became her lifeline.

"There were so many nights when I would call the hotline because I was so scared," said Horneman, now living with Mr. Puff, her daughter's cat, in a secluded condo in Plantation.

"Women In Distress provides hope. They attacked the whole problem, not just a piece of it. They are out there trying to help, to educate."

Women In Distress hopes to increase education programs in public and private schools because teenagers are the fastest-growing segment of domestic violence victims, said Andrea Bradley, the nonprofit's president and chief executive officer.

The Palm Beach County affiliate, Aid to Victims of Domestic Abuse, provides similar services to Palm Beach County residents.

The agencies take a holistic approach, including classes and treatment for the batterer as well as the victim.

Nancy Horneman wishes her husband had taken those classes.

Walter Horneman occasionally hit Nancy when they dated, but she was in love so she didn't worry about it, she said.

They got married and had Stephanie, their "miracle child" because Horneman didn't think she could get pregnant. Little Gus came two years later.

Walter Horneman, a recovering alcoholic, stopped drinking during most of their marriage, but he became increasingly abusive after Gus was born.

Horneman felt she did everything wrong in her husband's eyes. She said he would hit her for leaving a clean spoon on the counter, or for forgetting to line up canned foods in alphabetical order in the cupboard. He monitored her phone calls, even to her mother, and threatened her if he had any inkling she wanted to call for help.

When her husband fell back into drinking binges, she learned to ride the waves in her tumultuous household and carve out happy spots.

"When Walter was out of the house, the house came alive," she said.

Horneman finally couldn't take it any more. On New Year's Eve 1998, Walter drunkenly stumbled into the garage to smoke a cigarette. Gus, 2, was asleep in his crib. Stephanie, 4, was at a relative's house.

"I told him he had to leave and he just looked at me and didn't say anything," she said.

When she took a step to walk away, her 6-foot-2, 200-pound husband grabbed both her arms, yanked her back, then grabbed her neck with both hands and slammed her into a wall two rooms away, she said. He beat her for several minutes and knocked the phone from her hands as she tried to call 911, she said.

For the next eight months, Horneman struggled through a separation and divorce. Her husband constantly tried to move back into the house. But through education and training by Women In Distress, she was able to say no.

Horneman filed for a restraining order against her husband, although she said he was able to stalk her at night without breaking the order because he had the right to use a car they shared. He also had full rights to see his children because a judge ruled he had not harmed them, Horneman said.

It was Walter's turn to keep the children on a Friday in August 1999. When she called him to discuss picking up the children on Sunday, she realized he was drunk and decided to send the police to his apartment instead.

When police arrived they found Stephanie and Gus dead, tucked neatly in their beds. Walter had asphyxiated the children, according to toxicology reports. He had then hanged himself with fishing wire.

For months that turned into years, Horneman said she struggled to understand her husband's actions, why he felt he had to kill. She found out only at his funeral that he was a victim of abuse as a child.

"The reason why he took their lives is because in domestic violence, the children become nonhuman," Horneman said. "They were his tools to get to me."

She started collecting angel figurines, pictures of angels, anything with angels, to help soothe her pain. Being alone was her biggest struggle. Horneman found that when she was alone, the horror sank back in over and over.

CHAPTER FIVE

So she became more active and accepted the helping hands offered to her. Horneman said Women In Distress and a counselor with her employee assistance program at work empowered her to mourn her children and get to know herself.

Now Horneman, a teacher, speaker, successful businesswoman and independent associate for Pre-paid Legal Services, shares her story with abuse victims nationally. She points out they are "women, men, gay and straight."

She hopes to start a foundation in her children's names for domestic violence victims who are forced to start over on their own, without financial help.

"You can either let fear stop you in your tracks or use it as fuel. I chose to use it as fuel," said Horneman. "I realize I must have been left behind for a reason. If I can save one life by telling one story, the kids didn't die in vain."

Karla Shores can be reached at kshores@sun-sentinel.com or 954-356-4552.

ABOUT THE AGENCY

For every family or person featured in Sun-Sentinel/WB39 Children's Fund stories, there are many in need. The agency spotlighted today, Women In Distress, wants to help more of them. Serving South Florida for 30 years, Women In Distress began as a four-bedroom home on Sistrunk Boulevard and gradually grew into a thriving agency that offers 62 beds in confidential locations throughout Broward County. The agency offers counseling, legal aid and job training, as well as a volunteer program and a thrift store. A Palm Beach County affiliate, Aid to Victims of Domestic Abuse, provides similar services to Palm Beach County residents. The hotline number for Women In Distress is 954-761-1133. For general information call 954-760-9800 or visit their Website at www.womenindistress.org. The hotline number for Aid to Victims of Domestic Abuse is 561-265-2900 or 1-800-355-8547. For general information call 561-265-3797.

Contributions to the Sun-Sentinel/WB39 Children's Fund will make it possible for local nonprofit agencies to serve needy children and families by providing grants for food, shelter, health care,

> abuse prevention services, educational and cultural programs — even toys for the holidays. All administrative costs are paid by the South Florida Sun-Sentinel, WB39 and the McCormick Tribune Foundation, which contributes $1 for every $2 donated.
>
> To contribute, please call 800-381-2112 or visit www.sun-sentinel.com/childrensfund.
>
> Copyright © 2004 Sun-Sentinel Company.

There are countless stories I can share with you, but I think you understand now, you are not alone.

The moral to these true stories are, you need to let go of the devil for the other angels to come through. And even if the angels never appear ... you have the best angel ever right by your side, YOU!

CHAPTER 6

PART ONE
Finding Yourself

You need to find yourself. Find a counselor, call the hotlines, I really can't stress this enough and know you are going and calling because you need to vent all your feelings to someone that doesn't know you or your partner. You need a third party to be an ear for you, not to judge or give their opinion (at least not right away).

Every day is another day of healing, and understand, you will never be 100% completely cured, however, there is life after abuse. You will learn how to carry on and live a great life.

You see, I firmly believe and know from my own personal experience, that everything we go through in life and everything that happens to us is for a reason. It is called, "Life's Lessons."

The older we get, the wiser we become because of what we go through personally and as long as you are willing to take charge of your life and you are willing to change, you will know what you want and you will be stronger so you never allow any abuse to happen to you again. You will choose what is acceptable and what is unacceptable behavior toward you by your future partner(s) and others. Again, with this being said, it all starts with you taking charge of you. Are you ready to start right now and just do something small before you go to bed tonight? OK ... do it! (What have you been wanting to do for you ... but haven't?)

Every day, start changing things a little at a time. This is called the Slight Edge ... step out of your comfort zone and do a little every day. It doesn't have to be big, it can be as small as waking up and starting your day differently. Maybe if you don't wear makeup but wish you look prettier ... put some mascara on and get dressed for you. LOL ... Have you seen what many of the actresses and entertainers look like before makeup that you wish you looked like, g's. If you normally wake up and you drag yourself through the morning, maybe you will want to start the beginning of your day with a shower and getting dressed as if you were meeting someone for a casual lunch. Do what makes you feel good so when you look in the mirror you are starting to see a brighter you.

Just do a little something new every day for you. Baby steps. Sica would ask me, "Why are you putting on makeup and getting dressed when you aren't going anywhere?" ... my response ... "For me, no one else, just for me." It makes me feel better about me. I didn't get dressy dressed, it was probably just jeans and a nice shirt. But I decided I would wake up every morning and take care of me first and then the rest of the day will follow. Same thing in the evening, at the end of my day, I would take a shower and maybe just put some mascara on, my daughter asked me "How come? You're not going anywhere," my reply ... "Just for me, that's all, just for me." And whenever I would pass by a mirror, I would see someone I liked. I would read or listen to personal development, write in my journal and relax. Then the next day, I would choose something else ... maybe going somewhere alone when I've never done that before. To the movies was a good start. Just do a little every day to help you become a better you for you.

Hey, do you like to dance? Good dancer, bad dancer, it doesn't matter. Here is what I did: I love to dance, but I hated going out to clubs because I didn't want to dance with anyone, so I found country music and discovered line dancing where you don't need a partner and no one touches you and you don't have to worry about getting picked up. You don't need anyone to go with you, just go by yourself. After all, you are your own best friend and who better to share this with, but you.

Oh my G-D, It's great, I would go, take the lessons with everyone and then dance with everyone in a line. (Most country bar clubs offer line dance lessons before it is open dance.) Maybe you will want to try this. It's not only good exercise for you physically, but also mentally and it is FUN! You start meeting new people as well. I met a few new friends and now when I went, I knew some people! This was getting to be a lot of fun! I was going two or three times a week and most of the time just staying for the lesson and maybe one or two line dances, spent about two hours there so it was like going to the gym, great workout and I loved this!

FYI ... I would drink water or coffee most of the time.

This is so important, learning about you and that you can do anything you want by yourself. I guess the biggest thing for me was to realize I can do things alone and I didn't need anyone to have a good time.

So with that being said ...

Every day ...

PART TWO
Personal Development – Refer To The Beginning Of This Book

Do your *daily exercises* for yourself every day. It's called the *Slight Edge* theory ... They are easy to do *and they are* also easy not to do ...

"*Successful people do what unsuccessful people are not willing to do,*" in other words, as long as you are willing to step out of your box,

CHAPTER SIX

even if you don't accomplish the results you wanted, you will have learned something from it and you will grow from it and become a better you. It is called failing your way to the top ... But these are good failures.

Start making a difference everyday for you, so you will find the greatness within yourself, because you do have GREATNESS WITHIN! I can't tell you how many things I've experienced and the results were not at all what I thought they would be, but I learned from them and I just moved forward.

1) *Personal Development* is huge just like I've stated in the book.

    Definitely, read ten pages a day of a good book on positive motivational self-help and/or listen to an audio for fifteen minutes that makes you feel good about yourself. I can't stress this enough; read a good book and/or listen to good motivational audio tapes.

Personal Development will help you in so many ways, from the way you look at yourself as well as things you can accomplish ...

Watch some recordings of Motivated Speakers (There are many to choose from.) (www.youtube.com).

I have many favorites, but when I was going through my hardest times, it was none other than Mr. Les Brown that I watched and listened to and read.

And every night, in your brand new journal, write down

what your new accomplishment(s) were for the day and what you want to do new for yourself tomorrow. A journal is a great way to also stay in touch with you.

CHAPTER 7

PART ONE
And Through My Journey

The best chapter is finally here and I know so many more will follow ...

Today in the year 2008, 22 years later, my life is so complete. It took me 20 years to find the man of my dream. I refused to settle for happiness, I finally like who I am and I wasn't ever going to get married again ... I never believed in a million years, that I would ever find anyone that I would want to spend the rest of my life with, let alone marry. I wasn't looking nor was he and here we are today, Lyn-Dee and Mark, happily married to each other and we truly are each other's best friend.

I found someone that loves me for me, that accepts me for who I am and doesn't try to change me, no matter how off the charts I can be and those that know me, truly understand Lyn-Dee and my -ism's. It's all Good! LOL.

We have a wonderful family that you read about in the beginning of this book and we do have our fair share of normal family problems, but we are a whole and an amazing support for each other.

Today, I am very secure, very positive, very confident … but every now and then, I don't know why or how … the insecure woman comes out in me and I get scared and sometimes just want to cry … even though things are great. *(This is why I said earlier – you will never be 100% cured.)*

Life Is Good!

"Do you believe?"

The question is … "Do you believe?" Because it can happen for you too … you are someone special and you deserve everything and more … sometimes, it just takes a *long time* to get there, but when you get there … it's a WOW! And what if you don't find your dream partner … SO WHAT … you have you and that is all you need. Learn about you and enjoy life to the fullest; there are many things to do and see and they are all wonderful. *I found me before* Mark and I found each other. All I needed and wanted was for Sica and I to be OK and I knew the rest would follow.

WARNING

VERY STRONG LYN-DEE-ISM!

TURN THIS PAGE AT YOUR OWN RISK

OR

JUST TURN THE NEXT PAGE WITH THIS ONE TO AVOID VIEWING!

CONTENTS: SEX

Warning ...
Crazy Lyn-Dee-ism – this might offend ...

Get to know yourself every way you can. You should never need a partner EVER. You should always just want one.

Just for one moment I will talk about sex and how to relieve the desire of searching for love in all the wrong places ... Now that's just wrong and not at all necessary to do.

Ready ...

... go to an adult novelty store and buy some toys, x-rated movies and learn how to please yourself. That, a glass of wine, (or whatever your flavor is), good music and the right setting and your favorite pillow ... will set you free.

EPILOGUE

*Y*ou *D*eserve *G*reatness and *Y*ou Can *L*ive

*M*y final thoughts to you …

Don't be a victim anymore, become that better you … a stronger you and believe that you are someone special … because YOU ARE! Haven't you had enough? Don't you feel lost and cried out? Isn't it time to strip the problem that causes you this grief and pain away from you and begin your life as you deserve to live it? It might be your time and it might not be, no one is judging you and no one is rushing you to do anything you are not ready for, I just hope I have given you the vision that when you are ready, you can start your life … when you are ready. Please allow me just to say this to you ... life is too short, don't wait too long or you are going to find yourself wishing you didn't waste all that time with the person who is your worst enemy, who is wearing the ... 'I care about you, I love you, nice guy disguise ...'

It might be scary at the beginning, oh hell ... it is very scary at the beginning, learning how to let go and start to learn about you, learning how to live alone without the ones that hurt you all the time, that say you can't do anything without them. It is time to raise your kids in a home where there is love and security, not loud noises that hurt their hearts ... it is time to kick the person that is causing you pain to the curb, but you need to have a plan so you don't get hurt and have it thought out step by step ... You can do it. And even if you don't have kids, do it for yourself.

Just be safe and have direction and a path. I hope throughout this book, it has helped you develop your direction and a path to a fuller, happier life. Being alone isn't so bad, I promise. Don't misunderstand me, it is not easy at first, but you will get to know you, like you, and realize you are AMAZING and *pleasant* and *pretty wonderful* AND *capable of doing so many things*. So, I shared me with you ... to inspire you to go towards the light of freedom and keep going without ever looking back. You are the next Survivor.

Cheers to your future!

EPILOGUE

Poem

This poem is close to my heart. It was written by my daughter, Sica.

One Day

One day I wish to bury my past,
one day I pray moments of happiness would last.
One day I imagine shedding no tears,
one day I hope to carry no fears.
One day I want to cherish being alive,
and one day soon I know it will arrive.

One day I ask when I turn out the lights,
that One day I will discontinue crying at night.
for this night I choose to get over my sorrow,
for this night I will find a way to make
"my day" tomorrow.

If I don't change, things will remain the same
with my "I want" attitude, I have nothing to gain
I may never forget, but I can always move on
and my wishes, I wished for, will be
granted at dawn.

~~ *Sica* ~~

Your Self-Help Notes

Your Healing Self-Help Exercise

And now that you are at the close of this book, I want to first of all, thank you for allowing me to pour myself into you and remember, you are never alone. We are all here together. (Please use the hotline references in the back of this book or go online and find the closest one to you).

By now, I hope you are ready to at least take that first step and then one step at a time, to start your new chapter of life and when you look in the mirror, you see the new image that is the reflection of you … and you are starting to see the you … you've been looking for. one moment at a time … one day at a time …

Your Self-Help Notes

PRESCRIPTION

Day 1 And Then After

*W*ake up every morning and take your shower and get dressed for the day and look good for you and nobody else but you. Make that decision that today is the first day of the rest of your life and you are going to KICK BUTT! Work on the goal you set for yourself in your journal last night. Do something different today and tomorrow you will set another goal and/or continue to work on a goal you set. And every day, you will become stronger and stronger.

Suggestions: While you're getting ready for your day, in the Morning ... And in the evenings before you go to bed and while you are writing in your journal ...

Morning...

Mary J. Bligh's, "Just Fine"

OK ... It's Time to ...
Look into the mirror and see who you are right now ... take a good look, You are looking great this morning!

Look into your eyes and speak to your image out loud ... I am Someone that is INCREDIBLE, BEAUTIFUL, AMAZING AND SPECIAL I can and will ***** (set a goal for the day and it doesn't have to be a big one, just set a goal for the day and say it to yourself right now)

I CAN DO ANYTHING I SET MY MIND TO DO!

NOW, LET'S GO MAKE IT ONE HELL OF A DAY!

And in the Evening Before Bed ...

Look into the mirror and see who you are right now ... take a good look, (and say this to yourself out loud ...)

YES! I have accomplished the goal I set for myself (or) I came closer to it than I ever have before (say the accomplishment out loud)

GREAT JOB! Don't you feel proud of yourself? I do.

Listen to "Dream Big"

PRESCRIPTION

while you are writing in your journal, ... look into the mirror and look into your eyes and tell your image ... I am Someone that is INCREDIBLE, BEAUTIFUL, AMAZING AND SPECIAL I did ***** (state your accomplishment) And tomorrow I will ... (state your goal for tomorrow)

I CAN DO ANYTHING I SET MY MIND TO DO

I hope by now, when you go back to the mirror and look at yourself, you believe in yourself more then you did when you started this book. And you are ready to enjoy your new journey of life ...

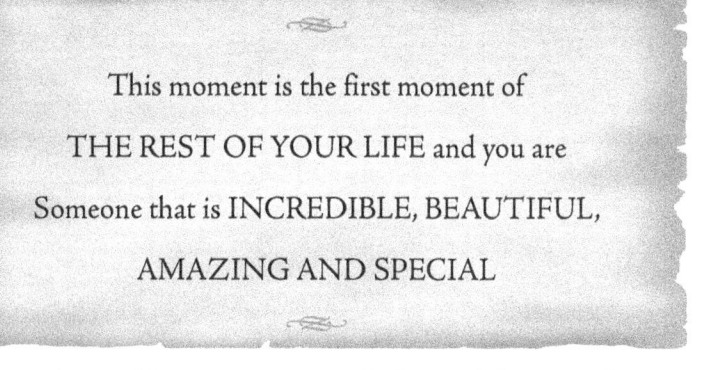

> This moment is the first moment of
>
> THE REST OF YOUR LIFE and you are
>
> Someone that is INCREDIBLE, BEAUTIFUL,
>
> AMAZING AND SPECIAL

You can do anything you set your mind to and the rewards are pleasant and powerful for you within...

You have now been found! Now Follow the Light!

Please make sure you are reaching out for help using a counselor and/or hotline.

Your Self-Help Notes

Your Daily Exercise

AND NOW ... Here are your daily exercise routine that you should follow and try to never miss a day

♡ Listen to the songs that inspire you ♡

1 In the morning do your mirror exercise

2 Read and/or listen to Personal Development

3 Do something different for yourself today

4 Before bed, do your mirror exercise

5 Read and/or listen to Personal Development

6 Write in your journal while listening to inspiring music

Your Self-Help Notes

LEGAL HELP

*T*here *I*s *H*elp *F*or *Y*ou

(This is not an advertisement)

*P*lease allow me to share with you a service that is available to all of us, but most of us don't even know it exist.

The bottom line is whenever we are in any kind of situation, especially like this one, it is always good to have an attorney you can speak to. It is important that you always know what your rights are and how you should handle things so the law is on your side. I haven't found a better way to do this then PRE-PAID LEGAL SERVICES,® INC. AND SUBSIDIARIES.

I am just sharing this information with you and you do whatever you want with it. Just know there is help. I wish this was available for me back in the day.

Whenever you are going through your disputes, your abusive partner is going to say things to you that if you don't know what your legal rights are at all times, you will not know how or what to do about it. You will feel alone and trapped ... NOT ANYMORE. Now you can for a small monthly membership fee, always speak to an attorney and be ahead of the game.

Examples:

You can't have the kids ...

You are going to leave with nothing ...

it is all mine ...

etc, etc, etc ...

With a Pre-Paid Legal Membership, you will be able to speak with an attorney for unlimited number of personal or business matters and never worry about how much it will cost you every time you need to just speak to an attorney.

Protect Your Rights!

I became a member of PRE-PAID LEGAL SERVICES,® INC. AND SUBSIDIARIES seven years ago and it was incredible to be able to have access to attorney's and always know what to do about different situations and how to handle them.

The service was so good that I have been an Independent Associate for Pre-Paid Legal for over seven years and now help people nationwide.

LEGAL HELP

When you need an attorney, you'll be really glad you have Pre-Paid Legal. Any time you have a legal problem or question, you can have access to quality law firms nationwide. With a Pre-Paid Legal membership, the services of quality attorneys are just a phone call away.

Skeptical? I was too. (Note: the unlimited phone consultations are only one part of the membership, there is much more to it).

Again, you can have access to the justice system to always know what your legal rights are and how to handle and deal with situations. For more information, please go to my web site below, click on the first sub-division, Family Legal Plan, and view the short 5-minute movie. If you have any questions, please contact me through my site by e-mailing me. (make sure you are on my site, you will see my name in the upper left hand corner, Lyn-Dee Eldridge. I will reply. www.prepaidlegal.com/hub/lyndeehalenar

And if you just want to reach out and vent, I am here for you. Please let me know you are connecting with me through this book. You can go to my website: www.tearsfears.com

Your Self-Help Notes

APPENDIX

PART ONE
APPENDIX

The National Domestic Violence Hotline
web site: http://www.ndvh.org

If something about your relationship with your partner scares you and you need to talk, call the National Domestic Violence Hotline at:
1-800-799-SAFE (7233) or 1-800-787-3224 (TTY).

At the National Domestic Violence Hotline ...
We believe that every caller deserves to be treated with dignity and respect. We believe that every family deserves to live in a world free from violence. We believe that safe homes and safe families are the foundation of a safe society.

Until the violence stops, the hotline will continue to answer ... One Call at a Time. Help is available to callers 24-hours a day, 365 days a year. Hotline advocates are available for victims and anyone calling on their behalf to provide crisis intervention, safety planning, information, and referrals to agencies in all

50 states, Puerto Rico and the U.S. Virgin Islands. Assistance is available in English and Spanish with access to more than 170 languages through interpreter services.

If you or someone you know is frightened about something in your relationship, please call the National Domestic Violence Hotline at 1-800-799-SAFE (7233) or TTY 1-800-787-3224.

PART TWO

This page is sponsored and maintained as a volunteer effort of *The Paladin Group*.

Domestic Violence Agencies on the Internet Sponsored by
  The Paladin Group – Grant Mentors
  Domestic Violence Hotline Numbers by State
    http://www.ndvh.org/

ALABAMA

Alabama Coalition Against Domestic Violence
Provides a listing of agencies in various cities and counties.
P. O. Box 4762 ♦ Montgomery, AL 36101
Phone: (334) 832-4842 ♦ Fax: (334) 832-4803
http://www.acadv.org/

The Domestic Violence Intervention Center
The Domestic Violence Intervention Center (formerly known as East Alabama Task Force for Battered Women) is a non-profit organization that is dedicated to providing support and referral to victims of domestic violence in Lee, Chambers, Tallapoosa, Randolph and Macon counties in Alabama.
Safehouse: (334) 749-1515
Toll-Free Hotline: (800) 650-6522

APPENDIX

ALASKA

The Alaska Network on Domestic Violence & Sexual Assault

The Alaska Network on Domestic Violence and Sexual Assault (ANDVSA) is a statewide coalition made up of twenty-one domestic violence and sexual assault programs. The Network is committed to the elimination of personal and societal violence in the lives of women and children. The ANDVSA website, has contact information for 21 local domestic violence and sexual assault intervention programs throughout Alaska. Visitors can also find a Calendar of Trainings; local, national and international news; links on the web; and information about the ANDVSA STOP Violence Against Women Legal Advocacy Project.
Phone: (907) 586-5643

CALIFORNIA

San Diego Domestic Violence Council ♦ San Diego, CA

Provides resources, links and police contacts, and link with YWCA domestic violence help.
1200 Third Avenue, Suite 700 ♦ San Diego, CA 92101
Phone: (619) 533-6245 ♦ Fax: (619) 533-5507
Toll-Free Hotline: (888) 305-SAFE (305-7233)
http://www.sddvc.com/

YWCA ♦ San Diego, CA

YWCA-San Diego provides comprehensive programs and services for survivors and their abusers including sliding scale counseling, educational and support groups, shelter services and other programs geared to the abatement of domestic violence. The YWCA Counseling Center is part of the Domestic Violence Research and Training Institute/ Counseling Center site in the Pacific Beach Area. The Center is located just off Interstate 5 and can be reached easily by car or bus.
2550 Garnet Avenue ♦ San Diego, CA
Phone: (619) 239-0355
24-hour Hotline: (619) 234-3164
Toll-Free Hotline: 888-305-SAFE
http://www.ywcasandiego.org/

The Women's Refuge ✦ Berkeley, CA
Families who come to us for service are homeless for many reasons. The majority of these families are victims of domestic violence. We provide safety and security that allow these families to deal with the many issues that are involved in these situations.
P. O. Box 3298 ✦ Berkeley, CA 94703
Phone: (510) 547-4663

The Sparrow Foundation ✦ Colton, CA
To provide a loving, safe Christ-filled home that meets the physical, emotional, and spiritual needs of women and their children who have been victims of domestic violence. To use all means necessary to assure a safe environment for the resident women and children. To provide abused women with medical help and vocational training. To help abused women and their children with emotional and spiritual healing through individual love care, counseling and prayer. To reach out separately to the abusive man and offer alcohol and drug dependency recovery and counseling with the goal of restoring families.
P. O. Box 2253 ✦ Colton, CA 92324
Phone: (909) 783-8103
http://www.sparrowfoundation.org/

UCLA Men and Women's Resource Center ✦ Los Angeles, CA
Resources, information and telephone numbers for students in the UCLA area of Los Angeles and Santa Monica.
Box 951453 ✦ 2 Dodd Hall ✦ Los Angeles, CA 90095-1453
Phone: (310) 825-3945
http://www.thecenter.ucla.edu/

The Domestic Violence and Sexual Coalition of Nevada County, CA
Grass Valley and Truckee Crisis Lines

APPENDIX 109

Laura's House ♦ Orange County, CA
A shelter for Women and Children in South Orange County.
Phone: (949) 498-1445
24-hour Hotline: (949) 498-1511
E-mail: information@laurashouse.org
http://www.laurashouse.org/

Marin Abused Women's Services (MAWS) ♦ Marin County, CA
Marin Abused Women's Services (MAWS) provides emergency hotlines, housing facilities, support groups and a men's program.
Women's English Hotline: (415) 924-6616
Women's Spanish Hotline: (415) 924-3456
Men's Hotline: (415) 924-1070
http://www.maws.org/

Maitri ♦ San Francisco, CA
Maitri is a free, confidential, non-profit organization based in the San Francisco Bay Area that helps South Asian women facing domestic violence, emotional abuse, or family conflict. We provide peer support and referrals to legal help, emergency shelters, and counselors.
http://www.maitri.org/

La Casa de las Madras ♦ San Francisco, CA
Offering Shelter, Advocacy, and Support Services to Battered Women and their Children.
Adult Hotline: (877) 503-1850
Teen Hotline: (877) 923-0700
http://www.lacasadelasmadres.org/

Domestic Violence Project of Santa Clara County, CA
Comprehensive resources, contacts, hotlines, and information for Santa Clara County. Includes educational/informational resources. They have over 1200 indexed links to Internet resources on violence, over 100 links to relevant online journals, art by victims and award winning editorial illustrators, a 4000 item bibliography, medico-legal protocols, battered women's stories with photos, downloadable posters, essays by youth, newsletters, and more.
http://www.growing.com/nonviolent/

Center for Domestic Violence Prevention ♦ San Mateo, CA

Offering in-house counseling and support services to residents in our shelter program. We are committed to ending the inter-generational cycle of violence.
Phone: (650) 652-0800 ♦ Fax: (650) 652-0808
24-hour Hotline: (650) 312-8515.

Women's Shelter Program ♦ San Luis Obispo County, CA

WSP offers two distinct programs. The first program, the Emergency Shelter Program, consists of the 10-bed safe house, which provides safe shelter, food, and clothing to victims and their children who are in immediate danger due to domestic violence. The Emergency Shelter Program also offers counseling to women and children, advocacy with legal services and social service organizations, and case management in order to help the residents establish violence-free and economically feasible lives after they leave the shelter.

The second program, geared toward domestic violence victims who are not in immediate danger, consists of support services. There are two main support services. The Center for Alternatives to Domestic Violence (CADV) is a sliding-scale counseling center, which offers individual and/or group counseling to any family member affected by domestic violence. CADV also offers some group counseling and accepts Victims of Crime (VOC) funds. There are several groups offered at different sites throughout the county. CADV offers a group for Spanish speaking women and lesbians experiencing domestic violence. Groups for children, teens, and women are also offered.

The second support services is the Legal Program, which consists of both a Domestic Violence Temporary Restraining Order Clinic and assistance with custody issues in domestic violence cases where the parents are unmarried. Potential clients of this program must meet certain income guidelines.
Toll-free Hotline: (800) 549-8989.
http://www.womensshelterslo.org/

Cornerstone Counseling Center ♦ Ventura, CA

Offers domestic violence counseling for batterers.

APPENDIX

COLORADO

Crossroads Safehouse ♦ Larimer County, CO

The mission of Crossroads Safehouse is to end family violence in Larimer County. Crossroads provides emergency shelter, counseling, and support services to victims of domestic violence.
24-hour Hotline: (970) 482-3502
http://www.crossroadssafehouse.org/

FLORIDA

Abuse Counseling and Treatment, Inc. ♦ Fort Myers, FL

Abuse Counseling and Treatment, Inc. is a non-profit organization founded in 1978 to assist victims of domestic violence and sexual assault. Services include emergency shelter, 24-hr. crisis hotline, advocacy, support groups, batterers' intervention program, and children's program.
24-hour Hotline: (941) 939-3112
http://www.actabuse.com/

Betty Griffin House ♦ St Augustine, Florida

St. Johns County's only Safety Shelter for abused women and children. Confidential counseling, legal assistance, community education, and a 24-hour domestic and sexual violence hotline. We also provide all services to men who are abused with separate accommodations.
24-hour Hotline: (904) 824-1555
http://www.bettygriffinhouse.org/

Refuge House ♦ Tallahassee, FL

Domestic Violence/Rape Crisis. Serving 8 Counties: Franklin, Gadsen, Jefferson, Leon, Liberty, Madison, Taylor, Wakulla.

The mission of Refuge House is to provide direct services to battered women, their children and sexual assault survivors, as well as to work to eliminate the conditions in society that allow such violence to continue.

Refuge House provides: Emergency Shelter, Counseling Programs, Injunction Assistance, Sexual Violence Program, Volunteer Opportunities
P. O. Box 20910 ♦ Tallahassee, FL 32316-0910

Phone: (850) 922-6062
24-hour Hotline: (850) 681-2111 Collect calls accepted

GEORGIA

Men Stopping Violence (MSV) ♦ Atlanta, GA

Men Stopping Violence (MSV) is a pro-feminist, private, non-profit organization based in Atlanta, Georgia dedicated to ending violence against women. MSV offers re-education programs for men wanting to change their violent and abusive behavior, training programs for concerned community leaders about how to intervene effectively, plus many other activities in the effort to put an end to violence against women. Also in Douglasville, Georgia.
http://www.menstoppingviolence.org/index.php

Citizens Against Violence (CAVINC)

Serving counties of Bulloch, Candler, Effingham, Jenkins and Screven, GA. A Transitional Housing (Next Step Program-Subsidized apartments to transition clients from emergency shelter to independent living.)
     Victim Support Groups (Support groups help victims recover emotionally and develop skills required to return to normal lives.) Outreach and Education (Informing the community about the problem, what services we offer, and how people can help us).
24-hour Hotline: (912) 764-4605
Outside Bulloch County Toll-Free: (800) 33-HAVEN (this statewide 800 number rings at the closest shelter)

HAWAII

Parents And Children Together (PACT) ♦ Pu'uhonua, HI

Provides counseling for victims of domestic violence, legal assistance, child care, evidence collection, and police intervention. Monday thru Friday 7:30 AM – 5:30 PM; a counselor is available at the Waianae Police Station until Midnight Monday through Friday.
Phone: (808) 522-5535
http://www.pacthawaii.org/

IDAHO

Idaho Domestic Violence Programs
This is a listing of many domestic violence programs in the State of Idaho.
http://www.co.bannock.id.us/dv24hour.htm

ILLINOIS

A Friends Place ♦ Chicago, IL
A free walk-in counseling center for women and children. Friends also provides a 24-hour crisis referral Hotline, court advocacy, and community education.
Friends of Battered Women and Their Children
P. O. Box 5185 ♦ Evanston, IL 60204
Phone: (773) 274-5232
24-hour Toll-Free Hotline: 1-800-603-HELP

Apna Ghar ♦ Chicago, IL
Apna Ghar is a domestic violence shelter serving primarily Asian women and children, and is the first Asian shelter of its kind in the Mid-Western United States. Apna Ghar takes its name from a Hindu-Urdu phrase meaning "Our Home", and since January 1990, it has served over 3100 domestic violence clients.
Contact Apna Ghar
4753 North Broadway, Suite 502 ♦ Chicago, IL 60640
Office: (773) 334-0173 ♦ Fax: 773-334-0963
http://www.apnaghar.org/indexnew.shtml

Women's Crisis Center Of Metro East ♦ Belleville, IL
We are a comprehensive agency offering a 24-hour crisis hotline, emergency shelter services, court and police advocacy, individual and group counseling, nursing services, art therapy and a prevention/education program.
P. O. Box 831 ♦ Belleville, IL, 62222
Belleville Hotline: (618) 235-0892
East St. Louis Hotline: (618) 875-7970
Chester Hotline: (618) 826-5959
Waterloo Hotline: (618) 939-8114
TDD (618) 233-0741 ♦ Fax: (618) 235-9521

24-hour Toll-Free Hotline: (800) 924-0096 Monroe/Randolph Co. only
http://www.vpcswi.org/

INDIANA

Non-Violent Alternatives Counseling Services ✦ Shelbyville & Indianapolis, IN
Provides counseling services. Web Page has educational information on non-violent parenting, etc. Browse site for information.
http://www.nonviolentalternatives.com/

IOWA

Council on Sexual Assault and Domestic Violence ✦ Sioux City, IA
The Council on Sexual Assault and Domestic Violence provides support, advocacy and a safe environment to empower adults and children who have experienced domestic violence or sexual assault. Through leadership and education, CSADV works collaboratively with the community to promote social change and end violence.
Phone: (712) 277-0131
24-hour Toll-Free Hotline: (800) 982-7233
http://www.safefromabuse.com/

MAINE

Caring Unlimited ✦ York County, ME
Caring Unlimited, York County Maine's Domestic Violence Program.
P. O. Box 590 ✦ Sanford, ME 04073
Office: (207) 490-3227 ✦ Fax: (207) 490-2186
24-hour Hotline: (207) 324-1802
24-hour Toll-Free Hotline: (800) 239-7298
http://www.caring-unlimited.org/

MASSACHUSETTS

Emerge ✦ Cambridge, MA
We are the oldest batterers intervention program in the United States. We run groups for heterosexual men, gay men, lesbians and

adolescents. We run groups in English, Spanish, Khmer, Vietnamese and Chinese.

We also provide extensive training in domestic violence and working with batterers. Offices in Cambridge, Quincy, Lowell, and Roxbury, Massachusetts.
2380 Massachusetts Avenue, Suite 101 ♦ Cambridge, MA 02140
Call (617) 547-9879 for information and directions to all locations.
http://www.emergedv.com/

Men's Resource Center of Western Massachusetts

The MRC has a wide variety of men's programs, including a batterer's treatment program.
http://www.mrcforchange.org/

Gay Men's Domestic Violence Project (GMDVP)

Founded in 1994 by a survivor of domestic violence, we are a grassroots, non-profit organization. We offer community education, emergency housing, a 24 hour crisis line, referrals, court advocacy, and information to allow gay, bisexual, and transgender men in crisis to remove themselves from violent situations and relationships.
GMDVP, PMB 131,
955 Mass Ave., ♦ Cambridge, MA 02139
Office: 617 354 6056 ♦ Fax: 617 354 6072
24-hour Toll-Free Hotline: (800) 832 1901
http://www.gmdvp.org/

Respond ♦ Somerville, MA

A safe place in a residential setting to give women and their children the opportunity to get away from abuse and begin to heal their lives. We house women and their children for eight weeks.
Individual counseling around the issues of abuse. We provide, by phone or in person, information on legal issues, welfare rights, the courts, restraining orders, housing and the names of other shelters.
Crisis Groups – A safe place to express feelings, to give and receive support from other battered women, and to explore alternatives.
Transitional Groups – A place for women who are out of crisis to discuss their lives, and to learn assertiveness, empowerment and communication skills.

Parent Education Groups – A confidential setting for survivors of domestic violence to discuss parenting issues. An understanding voice to give support and offer options in a time of crisis.
Domestic violence affects children too. These are groups where children can safely express their feelings and receive support.
P. O. Box 555 ♦ Somerville, MA 02143
Phone: (617) 625-5996
VOICE 24-hours, TDD 9 AM – 5 PM
Staff speak: Haitian Creole, Spanish, Portuguese and French.
Crisis Hotline/Direct Service Office: (617) 623-5900
24-hour Hotline: (617) 623-5900

Danvers Massachusetts Police Department

The Danvers Massachusetts Police Department page offers local information for Massachusetts residents, including current laws, police officers' duties regarding restraining orders, hotline numbers, local numbers to DA's Office, victims' rights, and more. They also have links to other sites as well.
Help for Abused Women and their Children (HAWC): North Shore of Massachusetts
Help for Abused Women and their Children (HAWC) provides comprehensive services to abused women in 23 communities on the North Shore of Massachusetts.
27 Congress Street ♦ Salem, MA
Phone: (978) 744-8552 ♦ Fax: (978) 745-6886
24-hour Hotline: (978) 744-6841
Gloucester 24-hour Hotline: (978) 281-1135
http://www.helpabusedwomen.org/

The YWCA of Western Massachusetts

The YWCA of Western Massachusetts has been serving the women and youth of our region for more than 130 years. We offer comprehensive domestic violence and sexual assault programs including: confidential 24-hour hotlines, emergency shelter, legal advocacy and referrals, individual counseling and support groups and community outreach.
Springfield, Westfield, Northampton, MA.

MICHIGAN

Safe Haven Ministries ♦ Grand Rapids, MI
The mission of Safe Haven Ministries, Inc. is to show Christ's love by providing shelter and services to abused women and their children and to partner with the faith community to recognize and respond appropriately to families affected by domestic violence.
3501 Lake Eastbrook Drive, Suite 335 ♦ Grand Rapids, MI 49546
Phone: (616) 452-6664
http://www.safehavenministries.org/

SAFE House ♦ Washtenaw County, MI
The Domestic Violence Project, Inc./SAFE House provides services for any person victimized in an intimate relationship who lives or works in Washtenaw County, Michigan.
24-hour Hotline: (734) 995-5444
TDD: (734) 973-2227
For services elsewhere in Michigan, call
24-hour Toll-Free: (800) 99-NO-ABUSE

MINNESOTA

The Harriet Tubman Center ♦ Minneapolis, MN
The Harriet Tubman Center serves all family members: men, women and children. Our work focuses on safe, healthy ways of rejoining families. If you are dealing with a crisis, we are available 24-hours a day.
3111 First Avenue South ♦ Minneapolis, MN 55408
Phone: (612) 825-3333 ♦ 8 AM - 5 PM
24-hour Hotline: (612) 825-0000

Cornerstoner ♦ Hennepin County, MN
Cornerstone is the domestic violence program serving south Hennepin County, Minnesota. Cornerstone's mission is to prevent domestic abuse. Cornerstone's services include emergency housing, transitional housing, family and criminal court advocacy, long-term one-to-one and group support for children and adults, and violence prevention services in community schools.
1000 East 80th Street ♦ Bloomington, MN 55420
Office: (952) 884-0376 ♦ Fax: (952) 884-2135
24-hour Hotline: (952) 884-0330

MISSOURI

Comtrea

Comtrea is a private, not-for-profit organization which provides a comprehensive array of services to Jefferson County and some specialized services to South St. Louis County, South St. Louis City, St. Charles, Lincoln, Warren, and Franklin counties. Services include counseling, shelter services, and substance abuse services.
227 Main Street ♦ Festus, MO 63028
Phone: (314) 931-2700 ♦ Fax: (314)931-5304
http://www.comtrea.org/

NEW JERSEY

Domestic Violence State Resources

This Angels in Blue page provides domestic violence resources throughout the State of New Jersey.
http://www.angelfire.com/ar/LRfuzz1/shelters/dvsrnj.html

NEW MEXICO

Women's Community Association ♦ Albuquerque, NM

The Women's Community Association, and one of the largest shelters in the country, effectively serve 100 beds at one time. We are located in Albuquerque NM and not only take referrals from all over our own state, but other parts of the country as well. We also have a transitional housing program to aid survivors in rent for up to 2 years. Please feel free to correspond with the Director of Marketing and Development.
http://www.wca-nm.org/

NEW YORK

Suffolk County Coalition ♦ Suffolk County, NY

The Suffolk County Coalition Against Domestic Violence provides hotline, shelter, legal assistance, and employment services.
P.O. Box 1269M ♦ Bayshore, NY 11706-0537
Office: 516 666-7181
Hotline: (516) 666-8833
http://www.growing.com/nonviolent/

Safe Horizon Services: New York City Area

Safe Horizon is a direct service, research, advocacy organization serving the five boroughs of New York City. We operate extensive community and court based services for domestic violence, sexual assault, rape, child abuse, and assault victims as well as survivors of homicide. We operate hotlines for domestic violence victims, crime victims, and immigrants and offer mediation services. Safe Horizon is committed to violence prevention and conducts school based programs for youth. Current innovative efforts include working with managed care organizations and corporations around the issue of domestic violence. We have information, research, and materials on victimization, victim rights, victim assistance, youth violence, and prevention. Save Horizon employs over 650 people in a variety of capacities from social workers to computer programmers. There are generally job openings in positions throughout the organization.

24-hour Crime Victims Hotline: (212) 577-7777
24-hour Domestic Violence Hotline: (800) 621-HOPE (4673)
TDD: (212) 233-3456 ♦ 800-810-7444

Rape, Sexual Assault & Incest Hotline: (212) 227-3000
New York Immigration Hotline: (718) 899-4000
  (Monday–Friday, 9 AM – 5 PM)

STOPline: (718) 596-1800

Elder Abuse Hotline: (212) 227-1227

Safe Horizon
2 Lafayette Street ♦ New York, NY 10007
Office: (212) 577-7700 ♦ Fax: (212) 385-0331
http://www.safehorizon.org/

NEVADA

SAFE House ♦ Henderson, NV

A community based, non-profit organization, committed to strengthening families by working to stop abuse in the family environment. SAFE House's programs include: Emergency Services (24-hour hotline, shelter, and community outreach); Family Transition

Counseling Program (Alternatives to Family Violence, Nurturing Alternatives, Alternatives to Aggression, Substance Abuse Treatment, and Family-Centered Case Management); and Family Strengthening Center (Nurturing Program, Family to Family Connection, and Coordinated Community Response).

NORTH CAROLINA

Domestic Violence Shelter & Services, Inc. ✦ Wilmington, NC

DVSS is located in Wilmington, North Carolina at a confidential location. We offer assistance to all victims of domestic violence and their children by providing emergency shelter, support groups, one-on-one peer counseling, children's services, and court assistance including obtaining protective orders. All services are confidential and at no cost to clients. One need not stay at the shelter to receive services. 24-hour Hotline: (910) 343-0703.

Randolph County Family Crisis Center ✦ Asheboro, NC

The Randolph County Family Crisis Center is in Asheboro, North Carolina, with a satellite office in Archdale, NC. We provide 24-hour crisis line; shelter for abused women and their children; court advocacy; rape crisis companions; support groups; abuser education program; parenting classes.
24-hour Hotline: (336) 629-4159 (also the administrative line).
Fax: (336) 629-0770
Archdale satellite line: (336) 434-5579
e-mail: jcarmc52@juno.com
http://business.asheboro.com/rcfcc/

NORTH DAKOTA

Domestic Violence Crisis Center (DVCC)

The mission of Domestic Violence Crisis Center, Inc., is to provide a full range of services to victims of domestic violence and sexual assault and also to reduce domestic violence by educating the public.
24-hour Hotline: 857-2200
Sexual Assault Hotline: 857-2500
http://www.minot.com/dvcc/

OHIO

Ohio Domestic Violence Network
Comprehensive list of resources by County.

OREGON

Bradley-Angle House ✦ Portland, OR
Bradley-Angle House was founded in 1975 as a domestic violence intervention agency and shelter program. Bradley-Angle House provides seven interactive components that serve and empower battered women and their children: 1) Emergency Shelter (a short term intensive program for 15 women and children); 2 & 3) Youth Programs (Shelter and Youth in Transition) (support and advocacy to young people staying at our shelters, or whose mothers are in Bradley-Angle House support groups); 4) Transition Program (long term case management, housing, advocacy, and support groups); 5) Outreach Program (support groups for survivors throughout the community and public education on domestic violence); 6) Crisis Phone Line (provides 24 hour peer counseling, resource referral and domestic violence information); and 7) Latin Program (ensuring access to all our services for Spanish speaking women).
24-hour Hotline: (503) 281-2442 (TTY Available)
http://www.bradleyangle.org/index.shtm

Raphael House ✦ Portland, OR
The mission of Raphael House of Portland is to provide a foundation of hope for a life free of family violence. Raphael House, in keeping with its Christian Philosophy, serves a diverse community of women and children escaping domestic violence and works to eliminate causes of family and intimate partner violence. This is accomplished by providing housing, case management, counseling, information and referrals, community education, and specially designed support services to enhance each housing program.
Office: 222-6507 ext.210
Hotline: (503) 222-6222
http://www.raphaelhouse.com/page/page/1852914.htm

Mid-Valley Women's Crisis Service ✦ Salem, OR
Mid-Valley Women's Crisis Service provides a safe environment for women and children survivors of violence.
Office: (503) 378-1572
24-hour Hotline: (503) 399-7722
http://www.mvwcs.com/

PENNSYLVANIA

Domestic Abuse Counseling Center ✦ Western Pennsylvania
The Domestic Abuse Counseling Center is a non-profit organization whose mission is to End Domestic Abuse in Western Pennsylvania. This mission is accomplished through the development of programs for counseling abusers; collaborative efforts with social service agencies, criminal justice systems, victim-advocate agencies, and health organizations; and by means of public awareness and education. The Domestic Abuse Counseling Center is committed to safety and justice for victims, attitudinal and behavior change of abusers, and non-abusive values in the community.
http://www.dacc.net/

Domestic Violence Services of Cumberland & Perry Counties (DVS/CP)
Domestic Violence Services of Cumberland & Perry Counties (DVS/CP) is a non-profit organization dedicated to providing services to victims of domestic violence and their dependent children in a two county area in Pennsylvania. Since its inception in July 1990, DVS/CP has served over 12,600 individuals with its 24-hour toll-free hotline, access to emergency shelter, individual and group counseling, legal and medical advocacy, and prevention education programs. All services are free and confidential.
Phone: (717) 258-4806 ✦ Fax: (717) 258-1677
24-hour Toll-Free Hotline: (800) 852-2102
http://www.dvscp.org/

Women In Transition, Inc. ✦ Philadelphia, PA
Women In Transition, Inc. has been in continuous operation since 1971 as a private, non-profit organization to empower women who are endangered by domestic violence and/or caught in the web of

substance abuse to find safety and sobriety. Services include 24-hour hotline, intake assessment, lifeline support groups, individual counseling, and community education. The Lesbian Intervention Project provides telephone counseling and support groups for women abused in same-sex relationships.
24-hour Hotline: (215) 751-1111
http://www.womenintransitioninc.org/

RHODE ISLAND

Rhode Island Coalition Against Domestic Violence
This page lists over several shelters and hotlines for domestic violence in Rhode Island.
http://www.ricadv.org/

SOUTH CAROLINA

South Carolina Coalition Against Domestic Violence & Sexual Assault
This page lists over a dozen shelters and hotlines for domestic violence in South Carolina. Many sources have web pages that are listed.

SOUTH DAKOTA

The Resource Center ◆ Aberdeen, SD
The Resource Center offers a wide variety of women's programs, especially counseling, education and crisis intervention. Programs include domestic violence and rape counseling, as well as crisis teams.
Phone: (605) 226-1212
Toll-Free Hotline: (888) 290-2935
http://www.safeharbor.ws/

TEXAS

The Rape Crisis Center ◆ San Antonio, TX
The Rape Crisis Center provides crisis counseling, advocacy and education in San Antonio, Texas.
http://www.rapecrisis.com/

The Women's Shelter ♦ Arlington, TX

The Women's shelter provides emergency shelter, independent living services, counseling and support groups, legal advocacy and crisis intervention.
24-hour Hotline: (817) 460-5566
http://www.womensshelter.org/

SafePlace ♦ Austin, TX

SafePlace exists to end sexual and domestic violence and abuse. SafePlace helps those hurt by this violence to heal and empower themselves. We provide prevention, intervention, education, and advocacy to our community so that women, children, and men may lead safe and healthy lives.
24-hour Hotline: (512) 267-SAFE
TTY: (512) 927-9616
http://www.safeplace.org/site/PageServer

VERMONT

Vermont Network Against Domestic Violence and Sexual Assault

Statewide. 24-hour hotline for domestic violence and for sexual assault. The Vermont Network can offer victims counseling and short-term advice, provide transportation to a shelter, and make referrals to other services. Currently, 16 different organizations are available through the Vermont Network umbrella, some dealing with sexual assault and some with domestic violence. The Vermont Network has a website with links to most of the other Vermont organizations.
24-hour Toll-Free Hotline: (800) 228-7395
24-hour Toll-Free Hotline for Sexual assault: (800) 489-7273
http://www.together.com/us/

WASHINGTON STATE

Washington State Domestic Violence Hotline

The Domestic Violence Hotline is a unique, statewide 24-hour toll-free hotline providing a spectrum of services to victims of domestic violence and their friends and families, including:
Crisis Advocacy – Trained advocates provide emergency assistance and emotional support and work with victims to develop alternatives to violence.

Information – Commonly asked questions including "Are my children learning to be violent by watching it?" *(yes)*; "Do I cause the violence?" *(no)*; "Is hitting me against the law?" *(yes)*; "Is there help available for me and my family?" *(yes)*

Referrals – Callers throughout Washington are put in touch with community and national resources respondent to the needs of victims of domestic violence.

24-hour Toll-Free Hotline: (800) 562-6025

WISCONSIN

Tri-County Council on Domestic Violence and Sexual Assault

Tri-County Council is located in beautiful northern Wisconsin with offices in Rhinelander, Eagle River, and Crandon.

Provides Temporary Shelter & Food, Peer Counseling Support Groups, Follow-Up Personal Advocacy, Legal Advocacy, including Restraining Order Assistance, Emergency Transportation, Community Education Information/Referrals, Judicare card issuing agency.

24-hour Toll-Free Hotline: (800) 236-1222
http://www.tri-countycouncil.org/

Wisconsin Coalition Against Sexual Assault

The Coalition provides links to a host of Sexual Assault Service Providers in Wisconsin. The following are services also provided by WCASA:

Resource Library – WCASA's headquarters houses the most comprehensive collection of books, journals, and videos on all aspects of sexual violence prevention, intervention, and treatment available in Wisconsin.

Training – We conduct several trainings each year, including large, statewide, multi-issue training institutes, as well as small site-specific trainings to meet the needs of community-based programs.

Publications – We produce Connections, a quarterly educational journal; fact sheets with current statistics, statutes, and general information; training and organizing manuals; networking directories; and membership newsletters.

Policy Development – Monitoring legislation that impacts survivors and service providers is another of WCASA's services. We also provide statewide advocacy and training to improve system and institutional responses to survivors of sexual assault.

Public Awareness – We conduct statewide annual awareness campaigns and are currently developing a statewide media campaign designed to educate communities in Wisconsin about sexual assault.
http://www.wcasa.org/

WYOMING

Directory of Wyoming Domestic Violence Programs

This Angels in Blue page lists agencies in the various Wyoming counties.
http://www.angelfire.com/ar/LRfuzz1/shelters/dvsrwy.html

AUSTRALIA, UNITED KINGDOM AND NEW ZEALAND

Victorian Information and Resources

Links to Men's and to Women's referral and domestic violence services in Australia.

Australian Drug Information Network

Linking people to a comprehensive range of websites and information resources on alcohol and other drug services in Australia.

Auckland Domestic Violence Centre ♦ New Zealand

Men's and Women's domestic violence services.
Domestic Violence Centre
P. O. Box 106 126
Downtown Auckland 1001 ♦ Aotearoa/New Zealand
Office: 64 9 303 3938 ♦ Fax: 64 9 303 0067
Hotline: 64 9 303 3939
http://www.dvc.org.nz/index.php?section=1

The Freedom Programme ♦ United Kingdom

A UK based 12-week rolling program. The Freedom Program assists women to recognize the tactics and beliefs of abusive men, to learn where those beliefs came from and which of those beliefs they share. They also run programs for abusers.

CANADA

Women in Second Stage Housing ♦ Winnipeg, MB

Residential Second Stage Housing Program for women victims of abuse and domestic violence. Women in Second Stage Housing is basically a one-year program for women with or without their children who are trying to leave abusive relationships and want to rebuild their lives and get on their own feet. Food bank is running every two weeks. W.I.S.H. offers counseling for women and children, life skills groups, Literacy Instruction, Coping Behavior Program, recreational and educational activities for families.

We can speak a number of different languages: Spanish, Chinese, Cantonese, French, and Punjabi.
St. Norbert ♦ P.O. 202 ♦ Winnipeg, MB, R3V 1L6.
Phone: (204) 275-2600 ♦ Fax: (204) 275-5416

Quetzal Family Homes ♦ Simcoe, ON

Quetzal Family Homes is located in Simcoe, Ontario and provides second stage housing for women and children who have survived abuse. Second stage housing is a safe, non-judgmental environment for women, with or without children, who have identified their own need for ongoing support and counseling. As well, second stage housing offers temporary, geared-to-income housing. These one, two, and three bedroom units include fridge, stove, and onsite laundry rooms. During their period of stay, participants make a commitment to focus on personal goals, work toward self-sufficiency, independence, and a life free of violence.

Hot Peach Pages and PATHS ♦ Canada-wide

These pages provide links to listings of almost 500 shelters across Canada, with a separate listing for Saskatchewan. There are also links to information on abuse against women, domestic and family violence. Helpful for victims, family, friends, doctors, lawyers, veterinarians, dentists. Listings include Domestic violence crisis lines, agencies for abused women, teens, seniors, and the disabled, plus information on battering, and links.